T0248477

THE

# TRADE ME
## PROJECT
### How a Bobby Pin Became a House

# THE
# TRADE ME
# PROJECT

### How a Bobby Pin Became a House

**DEMI SKIPPER**

Penguin
Random
House

**Publisher** Mike Sanders
**Editorial Director** Ann Barton
**Art Director** William Thomas
**Senior Designer** Jessica Lee
**Compositor** Ayanna Lacey
**Illustrator** Laura Robbins
**Proofreader** Mira Park
**Indexer** Johnna VanHoose

First American Edition, 2023
Published in the United States by DK Publishing
6081 E. 82nd St., Suite 400, Indianapolis, IN 46250

The authorized representative in the EEA is Dorling Kindersley
Verlag GmbH. Arnulfstr. 124, 80636 Munich, Germany

Library of Congress Catalog Number: 2022941415
ISBN 978-0-7440-7671-4

DK books are available at special discounts when purchased in bulk
for sales promotions, premiums, fundraising, or educational use.
For details, contact: SpecialSales@dk.com

Printed and bound in the United Kingdom

For the curious
**www.dk.com**

MIX
Paper | Supporting
responsible forestry
FSC™ C018179

This book was made with Forest
Stewardship Council ™ certified
paper - one small step in DK's
commitment to a sustainable future.
**For more information go to**
**www.dk.com/our-green-pledge**

## To Bobby

*Thank you for always supporting my dreams—*
*no matter how crazy they might be.*

# CONTENTS

# INTRODUCTION

I pride myself in being the kind of person who can just make things happen. The kind of person who can connect the dots to solve a problem—no matter what it is. The person who truly believes anything is possible.

For much of my life, people told me I had "Demi luck," like good fortune followed me wherever I went. For a while, I believed that was true: I'd just been in the right place at the right time. My successes were owed to that magical luck rather than considerable strategy and serious hustle.

As I got older, I realized luck had almost nothing to do with my achievements. I'd set goals that other people thought were crazy and then figure out the best way to achieve them. My philosophy has always been that nothing's impossible. With enough conviction, strategy, and planning, you can do anything.

Because of that belief, my life has been a series of side hustles and "make it work" moments. In third grade, I set up a jewelry business selling handmade pieces from my parents' front yard to a few neighborhood passersby. It went okay, but I knew there had to be an easier and faster way to make sales. Then I created my first eBay account. Because eBay required all users to be adults, I input my birth year as 1970 and my zip code as 02134. Neither of these were true; I wasn't born in the 70s, and my zip code wasn't the same as the PBS Kids show *Zoom*, but I was ready to do whatever it took to get that eBay account.

With this secret account, I felt like I'd unlocked the world. I could take pictures of the beaded bracelets I'd made, then plug my digital camera into my parents' desktop computer to create eBay listings for my jewelry. After the auctions ended, I'd package the bracelets and mail them to their new owners all on my own. I liked the cash I made from this, but I liked running my little business even more. This was my very first side hustle—the first of many.

This entrepreneurial attitude followed me into my academic and professional careers. I hustled my way into a job at Apple when I was stuck in an entry-level job designing car dealership bathrooms (really). I started business after business—some more successful than others—like custom lapel pins, wedding dress rentals, and laundry delivery (more on that later), all while working full time in tech. Then, while I was stuck at home during the pandemic, I began my craziest side hustle of all.

Inspired by a TED Talk, I decided it was possible to make a series of trades, starting with a bobby pin and working my way up to a house. This meant I'd have to convince people—one by one—to trade me their stuff until I'd traded my way to an entire home. It had been done once before, and I was convinced I could be the next person to do it. I didn't need luck—I just needed conviction and a serious set of strategies and skills.

This book recounts the story of the Trade Me Project and details all the tips, tricks, and strategies I used along the way. While this book is specifically about trading, the strategies are ones that can be repurposed for nearly any challenge you hope to accomplish—just one step at a time. My hope in writing this book is to give complete insight into how to make something entirely possible that might feel impossible.

# CHAPTER 1

# THE FIRST TRADE

In May 2020, we were two months into the COVID-19 pandemic lockdown. Like so many of us, I was spending all my time vacillating between my bedroom and living room, working over this new technology service called Zoom, and trying to find ways to fill my time. To be honest, that mostly meant watching a lot more TV than I ever had before. What else was I supposed to do now that I couldn't spend time with my friends or even leave my house?

One night, when I was especially bored, I got on YouTube and started doing that thing where you click on a video, watch it, and then follow the next random link. You can go down some pretty interesting digital rabbit holes that way. This is how I found myself watching a TED Talk (classic) given by a guy named Kyle MacDonald. Twenty years earlier, Kyle had undertaken a trading challenge: Starting with a paper clip, his goal was to trade each item until he finally traded for a house—and he'd done it.

I was fascinated.

My first thought was, *Is this for real?* (Yes, the Internet told me.) *If it was real,* I wondered, *why had no one else done it?* (No idea, said the Internet.) And right there in that moment, I decided: I'd do it. The next person to trade something small and meaningless using no money—just their ability to be strategic—until finally landing a real house would be me.

I told no one, not even my husband, Bobby. We'd gotten married only six months earlier, but he was already used to my wild ideas. When we first moved in together, I ran an enamel pin business, for which I made custom pins for restaurants and businesses. For one event, I (along with a friend I coerced to help me) packed more than 10,000 pins, causing the USPS to question why I was shipping six garbage bags full of tiny packages.

Later, I had a laundry business. I biked all over San Francisco picking up tablecloths and linens from fancy tech event spaces and washing them at home. It was backbreaking work and extremely low margins. Not my best idea.

During the pandemic, I'd even opened a wedding dress rental business so brides could have options for dresses even while all the stores were closed. This business worked out slightly better but still required us to hold an entire bridal shop's inventory in our tiny apartment. It also earned me some angry letters from a large wedding dress designer who didn't like the idea of people renting dresses instead of buying them.

Full disclosure: I have a real job. I'm a product manager at a technology company. Laundry and wedding dresses and the booming eBay jewelry business I ran out of my parents' basement when I was 11 years old have never been my primary source of income When I saw that TED Talk, I knew that if anyone could do it, it was me. Side hustles, crazy challenges, and figuring stuff out is in my DNA. Bobby wouldn't have been surprised or discouraging if I'd told him about my grand trading plan, but still, I kept it to myself. I wanted a little time to figure it out before I shared.

I closed my computer and got up. I needed my first item. I didn't want to fully copy Kyle MacDonald by also using a paper clip, so I walked around my house and looked at my stuff. I spotted a dollar laying on our console. *No*, I thought, *I don't want to use money.* This should just be about tangible items—no cash thrown in to sweeten the deal. But what?

I tried to find the smallest thing I owned, but it turns out size and value aren't perfectly correlated. For example, the rings I was wearing were small, but that didn't mean they were cheap. Neither was my phone nor my Apple TV.

Then, rifling through my drawers, I saw it: a pack of bobby pins. *One of these is worth—what? A penny?*

This was perfect. I opened the pack, took one bobby pin out, and held it in my hand. This would be the magical bobby pin that kickstarted my trading journey. Eventually, this bobby pin would become a house. At least, that's what I told myself, filled with excitement and enthusiasm.

*I should record myself. I need some way to keep track of all these trades I'll be doing,* I thought, getting way ahead of myself. I could always track the trades in a spreadsheet, but having videos where I showed the item and talked about what I was doing seemed way more fun—and easier.

I grabbed my phone and opened up this new app I'd downloaded: TikTok. I knew almost nothing about it. It had been getting a lot of attention during the pandemic, creating breakout stars and weird viral cat videos—the bread and butter of the Internet. I didn't think for a second that anyone would ever watch a single video I posted. I just wanted to keep track of my trades and create some kind of video record of my progress.

In order to upload a video, I first needed a username. I tried to think of what my TikTok handle should be. The whole purpose of the challenge was I wanted people to trade with me, so I came up with Trade Me Project. Simple and straightforward. I hadn't even made my first trade when I made my first video explaining who I was and my goal— to trade a bobby pin for a house.

Watching that video now, it's very clear I had zero idea what I was doing. People later left comments that the camera on my iPhone must have been dirty when I filmed it, given all the specks and fuzziness obscuring the bobby pin. Little did they know, it's not an iPhone video of a bobby pin. The video was actually shot on my iPhone, but when I couldn't figure out how to upload it to TikTok, I held my phone up to my computer and used its camera to film the iPhone video.

The quality of that video is so bad, it looks like it was filmed with your dad's camcorder in 1995, but again, I thought no one was going to see it. It was all of a few seconds—just some grainy footage of one little bobby pin. I uploaded my video, closed the app, and thought nothing else of it. Now I needed to make my first trade.

I began to brainstorm: Who'd want a bobby pin? Most likely women. How was I going to find women who wanted a singular bobby pin and, most importantly, would give me something for it?

Because it was the pandemic and I couldn't meet anyone in person, I'd have to use the power of the Internet. Given all my previous side hustles, a random Facebook group was a comfortable space for me. I joined a ton of Facebook groups where I knew most of the members would be women. My initial post went something like this:

*Hey, I have this dream to trade a bobby pin for a house. Here's an intro to me [link post to TikTok video] and the TED Talk that inspired me. If you'd be willing to trade, please let me know! -Demi*

I'll be honest: The initial interest wasn't high. Most people didn't get it. *I'm going to mail you something, and you're going to mail me a bobby pin? What's the point?* said every comment on my post. But as I'd discover time and time again later in this process, I just needed one person who understood and was willing to go along with my weird plan. For my very first trade, that was Abbie from Atlanta.

I found Abbie via a Facebook buy/sell/trade group where women exchange accessories and clothes. She saw my post and thought it was intriguing. I got a message on Facebook within an hour:

*Hi Demi! I'm super interested in doing this as long as you invite me to the house at the end.*

Abbie got me, and she got my dream. I was pumped. I'd done it! Someone else believed this was possible.

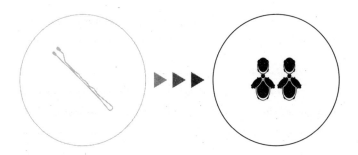

## TRADE 1: BOBBY PIN FOR EARRINGS

Now we actually had to negotiate a trade. I'd never traded for anything before, so I was kind of at Abbie's mercy. Whatever she was willing to offer me, I'd have to take. She also walked around her house looking for stuff and found a pair of earrings she'd been given for her birthday and never opened. ("I was going to donate them," she later told me.)

We agreed: my bobby pin for her pair of earrings. Abbie packaged up the earrings and mailed them to me; I packaged up the bobby pin and sent it to her. The initial steps of the trade were complete, and it had been much easier than I expected. While earrings that had been headed for the donation pile weren't a huge coup, it was a start. The only place to go was up.

About a week later, after checking my mailbox every day, the earrings arrived. They were from a brand called Marysol, a chandelier-style with pink plastic "stones" still on the original cardstock backing, new in their packaging and never worn. I made sure to film another video—this time using the TikTok app on my phone rather than recording my computer screen—to keep track of my progress. I once again uploaded the video and didn't think anything of it.

I'd done it. Trade 1 of the brand-new Trade Me Project was complete—as simple as that. I had no idea that with an insignificant bobby pin, I'd just taken the first step in a journey that would forever change my life.

# CHAPTER 2

# MARGARITA GLASSES AND TIKTOK FAME

A little-known fact about the Trade Me Project is I became TikTok famous before almost anyone in my life was aware of what was going on. Thousands of strangers were in on the Trade Me Project before even my husband was, and that was all thanks to TikTok.

The one person I'd told about my self-assigned challenge (other than thousands of Internet strangers) was my sister. The night before the Trade Me Project blew up on the Internet, I called her and explained my fun new hobby with its ambitious end goal. Start with a bobby pin—end up with a house.

"I don't know why anyone would do this or find it interesting," she told me, always supportive. "It sounds weird."

If you love brutal honesty, get a younger sister. (Credit where credit is due: She became key to the Trade Me Project later and is a huge cheerleader. Plus, she was half right—it *was* a weird challenge to undertake!)

Her reaction taught me the first valuable lesson of trading:

---

## Most people aren't interested in making trades.

---

Here in the United States and Canada, where I've done all my trades, trading or bartering is outside the norm. There are a few specific communities that engage in trading, but these are the exception, not the rule (more on this later). Culturally, we're used to cash as the medium by which to exchange value. If I want a new iPhone, I buy it at the Apple store with money. I don't show up at the Apple store with a Louis Vuitton bag and offer the sales associate the bag in exchange for a new MacBook Pro.

If you approach someone who's selling an item and ask them if they'd be willing to trade for it, you have to be prepared for a few reactions. Most likely, you'll be met with outright refusal. If you don't like rejection, trading isn't for you. You'll sometimes be met with rejection *and* annoyance for having wasted someone's time. That's the worst outcome. Best-case scenario: The person at the other end of the proposed trade wants exactly what you're offering them. Another workable outcome is they're open to trading, but they just might want something else.

## Potential Outcomes of an Offer to Trade

- Person rejects trading and is mad you asked

- Person rejects trading

- Person will trade but doesn't want the item you're offering

- Person will trade and wants your item

Or you blunt-force the trade, as I did for the second trade of the Trade Me Project. This isn't an approach I recommend, but it worked.

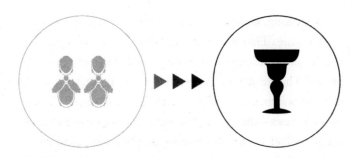

## **TRADE 2:** EARRINGS FOR MARGARITA GLASSES

There was some extra pressure on this trade, even though it was only the second one I'd ever done. That's because the day after I'd called my sister, I looked down at my phone and noticed something strange happening. I had a few notifications from TikTok announcing I had new followers. I'd totally forgotten I'd even posted that first video. Then I got more notifications. Then I got so many notifications that my phone almost crashed.

I remember this so clearly. I ran to wake up my husband, who was taking a nap.

"Something's happening!" I told him and showed him my phone. "I posted these videos and, I don't know, they're getting all these views and—"

"What videos?" he asked.

I explained—the project, my ultimate goal, using TikTok— and then we opened the app, or tried to. It crashed over and over again. Meanwhile, the notifications kept popping up.

All day long, we kept checking my account. The numbers were insane. That night, we had dinner outside with two neighbors who happened to be good friends of ours. We opened a bottle of wine and put my phone on the table so we could all watch. One million ... a million and a half ... These weren't views—they were followers. The Trade Me Project suddenly had 1.5 million followers. They wanted to know what would happened next. What would I even do with this kind of platform? It had absolutely not been part of the plan.

By the end of the night, I had *2 million followers*. That was 2 million people who thought I could do it or at least were committed to watching me try. The four of us finished the bottle of wine and were still absolutely shocked at what we had just experienced.

Getting started with my next trade was difficult, mostly because I had no idea what was going to come of this journey. All I had was the will to make it work. Fortunately, in the lower-value trades, strategy doesn't matter as much. One misstep won't make or break you. The second trade I made didn't hugely up-level my knowledge, but it did lay the foundation for trades to come.

While I was waiting for Abbie's earrings to arrive in the mail, I kept scouring the Internet for items that would work for my next trade. Now that millions of people were watching, the pressure was on. I also had a little time to think about how I wanted to approach the Trade Me Project. From the beginning, I'd set rules in mind I wanted to honor in my pursuit of the ultimate goal: trading for a house.

## The Rules of the Trade Me Project:

1. No using money to buy items or sweeten the deal
2. No trading with anyone I know

Using money to buy items or convince someone to take an item was the antithesis of the project. This was about direct exchange, not exchange using money as a proxy for value. Second, trading with people I knew seemed kind of fake. I wanted these to be real trades I found and negotiated, not a trade from a friend or family member.

From the beginning, I was relentless about the credibility and integrity of the Project—sometimes above and beyond what was probably necessary.

In the first half of Season 1 of the Trade Me Project, I also wanted to keep my Internet clout (once I had it) a secret. I wanted my success to be—in my mind—as pure as possible. Eventually, once the Project was big enough, this became impossible. But as it turned out, having Internet fame hurt way more than it helped (again, more on this later).

So, in pursuit of my second trade, I ventured back into the wilds of the Internet, trying to find someone who wanted to trade me for my new-to-me earrings. Rather than putting my item and story on the Internet and asking if anyone wanted to trade, this time I sought out items for which I'd be interested in trading. This was a small but critical shift in strategy. Rather than making people come to me, I'd go to them and convince them that trading was in their best interest—and mine.

This is how I found a set of margarita glasses on Facebook Marketplace. There were four of them made of clear blown glass with small air bubbles—the kind of thing you might find at a Mexican restaurant in Texas. They were nice (as I noted later in my TikTok), and I wanted them. Or really, I wanted to trade for them.

I immediately messaged the girl who'd posted them. Did she want to trade? I had earrings; she had margarita glasses. She explained she was happy to just give the margarita glasses away to a good home. Which is when I told her "No."

*You have to take the earrings*, I messaged her. *For trading. It's for a social experiment.*

*No*, she said, clearly confused and, as my sister predicted, weirded out. She didn't want the earrings. She was just happy to give me the margarita glasses. For free.

*I'm sorry, I need you to take the earrings!* I responded.

*No thanks*, she wrote me. *Where can I leave the margarita glasses for you?*

This was peak COVID, so we couldn't meet in person. She gave me her address and left the glasses on her porch. When I picked them up, I left the earrings. We never met each other in person. I wonder if she ever found out about the Trade Me Project or if she thought I was just some weird girl forcing earrings on her.

Getting the margarita glasses felt like a huge deal. I gave away *one* pair of earrings, and now I had *four* margarita glasses! I had successfully exchanged one item for four. The margarita glasses had been listed at $10. I wasn't sure about the value of the earrings at the time, but this felt like an increase in value to me.

I created a new video showing the progression from the bobby pin to the earrings to the margarita glasses. I got 1 million views in the first hour, then 1 million views in the second. By the end of the week, 10 million people watched it. Eventually, 30.6 million people liked it. That's more than the population of my home state.

If you look at the demographics of who watches my videos, they're very broad. Elementary school kids, 50-year-old moms, and millennial men all watch my videos. This is pretty unique, given that most videos on TikTok appeal to a specific demo. Maybe they have crossover value and hit two.

For people who aren't familiar with TikTok, the platform works by showing you a series of videos. If you like a specific video, TikTok will show you similar videos and also show the video you liked to people who share your demographics (hoping they'll also like the video). This is why we think the algorithm is so smart. TikTok quickly figures out what demographic you fit into and, based on that, what you'll probably like. You start to get slotted into certain related categories. And it usually does a creepily good job of predicting what you want to see. Your experience on TikTok will be totally different from your dad's, but it will probably look something like others from your demographic who live in your geographic region. People find themselves in content buckets—dancing videos + Glossier reviews + Olivia Rodrigo covers versus NASA launches + mountain biking courses + Bruce Springsteen concerts.

But from the beginning, the Trade Me Project has been lucky enough to have mass appeal. There's this joke I saw that everyone gets on TikTok and the first thing they see are videos of girls dancing (shout-out to the D'Amelios and Addison Rae!). If you swipe *no*, then you end up with dog rescue videos. If you swipe *no* to those, you're going to see a video of a girl trying to trade a bobby pin for a house. The Trade Me Project just became one of those core channels that TikTok pushed at people.

I think because the Trade Me Project was so ambitious but also seemingly simple—just trading one item for another—people resonated with it and really wanted to be there to see if I could successfully do it.

I knew I had something special on my hands, but I had no idea how big it would get. I was just focused on getting my next trade.

# CHAPTER 3

# SUPPLY, DEMAND, AND SNOWBOARDS

The first few trades of the Project happened quickly. Once I had the earrings in hand, it was just a couple days before I had the margarita glasses. I went back to my favorite place, the Internet, to find my next trade. While I was still in the low-value items, I'd learn several valuable lessons over the next few trades.

## TRADE 3: MARGARITA GLASSES FOR A VACUUM

To get started on my next trade, I began looking for items that people had priced in the $10 range on Facebook Marketplace in San Francisco. The earrings had taken so long to get to me—anyone remember what it was like mailing things during the early days of the COVID-19 pandemic?— that I was still spooked. I had intentionally chosen to look locally for the margarita glasses, and I did the same for this trade. I set the filters within a few miles of my location. From there, I started scrolling and sending out messages.

As I began looking at $10 items, I noticed there were lots of vacuums on the market. The vacuums came in all kinds of models at totally different price points. Some were really old and looked like they barely worked; others were top-of-the-market, brand-new Dysons that were definitely worth more than $10.

Maybe because there were so many vacuums on the market, people were having a hard time selling them. Did that mean they'd be open to trading? This is when I learned:

THE TRADE ME PROJECT

---

## If the market is oversupplied for their item, people are more willing to trade.

---

Trading the margarita glasses for the vacuum was one of the easiest trades I've ever made. I sorted the vacuums on Facebook Marketplace by posting date to see which had been available the longest, and a bunch of them had been there for months. People who had just listed their item might still want to hold out for money, but if their item had sat for months, maybe they'd be more willing to trade?

---

## If their item's been on the market for some time, people are more willing to trade.

---

Turns out, I was right.

I found an upright Bissell vacuum cleaner in my price range and contacted the girl who'd listed it. The listing was pretty stale, so I came prepared to negotiate with that as one of my talking points. As it turned out, I didn't even need my negotiation skills.

*Sure*, she messaged me right away. *I'd love to trade you.*

I hadn't even mentioned the Trade Me Project or pitched her on why the margarita glasses were worth so much more than the vacuum. She just wanted the glasses and had no problem trading for them.

We arranged to meet in person to make the trade, which was a first for me. I'd never met anyone I'd traded with before, but she was so enthusiastic, I couldn't say no. She and her partner drove up to our prearranged meeting spot. She hauled the vacuum out of her trunk, and I handed over the set of margarita glasses.

"Are you into crystals?" she asked.

I'd no idea what she was talking about, but I thought I'd better agree. Then she dropped several crystals into my hand—the kind of quartz and amethyst crystals you see in every celebrity's Instagram posts—no explanation included.

(You meet a lot of interesting people when trading.)

Now I had a vacuum *and* crystals. The crystals I put to the side. I didn't know if they'd be good luck, but they certainly weren't part of the original bargain. I started inspecting the vacuum I'd just traded for—and had my first moment of trepidation. The vacuum wasn't in great shape. It had scuffs all over and the top was duct-taped together. I knew it worked, but it wasn't pretty.

This is when I realized I needed to add a new rule to my list: If I traded for something and it had defects I hadn't specifically asked about or wasn't told about, that was on me. It was my responsibility as the person on the other end of the trade to ask all the right questions. Even if the vacuum didn't turn on, I couldn't message this girl and tell her we needed to reverse the trade. I'd be stuck with the vacuum, and it would be on me to figure out my next step.

On the other hand, when I traded an item away, I needed to be as up-front as possible about any problems it had. I could use every strategy I had to get someone to make a trade, but I could never misrepresent, mislead, or lie by omission when it came to the item I was trying to trade away. The description had to be extremely accurate so the other person knew what they were getting into. I truly had to believe the trade was a good deal for both of us.

## The Revised Rules of the Trade Me Project:

1. No using money to buy items or sweeten the deal
2. No trading with anyone I know
3. No tradebacks if I hadn't asked the right questions about the item
4. Always be 100% up-front about the item I was trading away

Was this crappy vacuum the end of the Trade Me Project? Was it over before it even started? It couldn't be. I had 1 million people watching me, and I had to make it work.

I couldn't spend money to have the vacuum repaired, but it wasn't against the rules to make improvements to the vacuum myself. I plugged the vacuum in, and to my relief, it worked fine. It just needed some TLC.

I started by investigating the duct tape wrapped around the top of the canister. When I removed the tape, I realized that it was holding the rear panel on the vacuum because a screw was missing. That was easy to solve. I got out my toolkit and found a screw of the right size. The missing screw must have been lost at some point because my new one screwed in just fine. Problem solved. The vacuum was already looking 80% better without the duct tape.

Then I examined all the scuffs around the bottom of the vacuum. Fortunately, the plastic itself wasn't damaged. The scuffs looked like they were just from some kind of paint or plaster. So I got out my nail polish remover and a rag and went to work. After 30 minutes, I'd completely polished out the scuffs. I don't want to brag, but the sad-looking vacuum I'd traded for looked brand new. We were back in business.

While the fixes were minor, I was proud of myself. I hadn't spent any money, but I'd totally upgraded my item! I'd added value and made my item more desirable to people. My bobby pin had become a functional and good-looking Bissell vacuum cleaner. Who wouldn't want it? I recorded another video in the same format I'd been using—explaining the inspiration for the Trade Me Project, showing my prior trades, and showing off the vacuum—and uploaded it to TikTok. The response was instantaneous this time. People were watching, liking, and commenting. I was finding my social media stride.

That is, until I started trying to trade the vacuum cleaner. I got back on Facebook Marketplace and started contacting people who had items of a slightly higher value than the vacuum. No one would bite. For the same reason the vacuum's original owner had trouble selling it, I was having trouble trading it. There were just way too many vacuums on the market, and most people already own a vacuum anyway.

What was I going to do? I was going to restrategize.

## TRADE 4: VACUUM FOR A SNOWBOARD

The success of the Trade Me Project is due in no small part to being able to use the power of the Internet. I've no idea how Kyle MacDonald did it back in 2006 without the abundance of social media platforms that are out there today. The idea of posting advertisements in the newspaper or cold-calling people sounds insane and admirable to me. I'd do it if I had to, but the Internet has made reaching people so much more efficient.

At this point in the Project, I'd only used Facebook and Facebook Marketplace to send out messages, but eventually, I'd be on every platform. (I'd also get banned and unbanned multiple times.) When I started looking for my new trade, I had no idea how many listings I'd have to go through before I nailed down my trade. Fifty? A hundred? Trade #4 gave me a taste of things to come, as I looked through a *thousand* trades before finding the right one.

Remember, I had—and still have—a full-time job as a product manager at a tech company. From 9 a.m. to 5 p.m.—and sometimes beyond—I'm working with my teams of engineers and designers to launch product features. At the time, I was working for a popular online restaurant reservations company, leading the development of their consumer app. They had no idea about the Trade Me Project, and given that it didn't interfere with my real job, they didn't care. Because the Trade Me Project has never been my full-time gig, I do all my trading totally outside my normal working hours.

(No, I don't sleep very much.)

Even by this time, I was already obsessed with the Project. I'd wake up at 6 a.m. every day thinking about my next trade. Then, from 6 a.m. to 8 a.m., I'd scroll the Internet and send messages to people, trying to get them to trade with me. During lunch, I'd look some more. Then, after work, I'd get back on my trading accounts and search some more. By the time I went to bed, I'd have spent *hours* every day working on my trade. Trading was a hobby, but from the beginning, I took it seriously.

Because I was still in low-value items, the range of what I could trade for was wide. I didn't really know what I wanted yet. All I knew so far was I didn't want more vacuums. What could I get for the vacuum? Tennis rackets? A skateboard? A set of workout DVDs from the 1990s? Scrolling Facebook Marketplace a few days after I had my vacuum, I spotted it: a snowboard.

The snowboard looked like it was in pretty good shape from the pictures, but I wasn't an expert in snow sports. It was a Dakine board sized for a guy and was a cool off-white and gray color. It came with the original bag, with a shoulder strap to transport it, which seemed like a plus. Something about it spoke to me.

I quickly looked up the profile of the person selling the snowboard. It was a woman in her fifties who lived about an hour from San Francisco. I carefully typed out yet another message, considering each word and the phrasing to make trading for my vacuum sound like the best idea she'd ever heard. I explained I lived in the Bay but that I'd happily meet her anywhere to trade our items. I had no idea why she was selling the snowboard, but I figured she might be interested in the vacuum.

*Sure*, she responded. *The snowboard is my son's. He's off at college, and he's not coming back for it. Can you meet me in [town] to exchange our stuff?*

This was just about in the middle of our two locations, which seemed fair.

*Absolutely!* I responded, even though my sole mode of transportation was a road bike.

I put down my phone. "Bobby, I have the next trade—but we have to rent a car *now*."

This is how I found myself in the parking lot of a McDonald's the very next day, Bissell vacuum cleaner in hand. My trading partner was already waiting for me. The only problem: It wasn't the woman I'd been messaging.

As I pulled into the parking lot, I spotted a middle-aged man holding a giant snowboard bag standing outside an SUV. I was immediately spooked. The woman had sent her husband in her place. It wasn't that I was worried he was going to *do* something weird; I was worried he was going to think this whole trading situation was so weird that he'd refuse to go through with it. I went into crisis mode, planning how I'd explain the situation to him so he didn't think his wife was getting scammed.

I wanted so badly to trade all the way to the house without disclosing the Project to people I was trading with, but this might be the moment where I had to change that tactic. I wasn't just some psycho who was randomly giving away vacuums, I'd tell him. There was a whole plan! I had a goal! I stepped out of the car and pulled out the vacuum cleaner.

"Hey, Demi," the man said. "Here's the snowboard. Thanks so much."

And that was it. Zero questions. Vacuum off to its new home—snowboard acquired. My luck was continuing to hold.

I was so excited about the snowboard. After having a hard time convincing anyone that the vacuum was a great idea, this seemed like an amazing trade. Bobby had a different take.

"That's really old," he told me.

He wasn't wrong—it wasn't the newest snowboard I'd seen listed for sale, but I'd chosen it strategically. I had a hunch that if I went for the nicest snowboard on the market, the person who had the money for top-of-the-market goods could probably just buy their own. By staying in the middle of the pack, I opened up more possibilities for myself by working with people who were already flexible on item type and value. This was a theory I'd really road test in the future once I got into items like high-end electronics and literal cars.

I was convinced *someone* would want this snowboard, and here I learned a valuable lesson that would apply to every trade I've made since:

---

**Beware of top-of-the-market items.**

---

## The Top-of-the-Market Trap

When looking for items to trade, try to stay away from items that are at the "top of the market." For example, there's a varying price range for items like drones. While it might seem advantageous to trade for the *very best* drone, it will actually be much harder to trade. Why is that? Simply because of supply and demand. Because there's a supply of many varying prices for drones, the number of people who'd be willing to pay less is high, and the number of people who see the value of the most expensive drone is low. I've found that most people would prefer to get a cheaper drone than one that's the best of the best.

This is especially true if the item is one not many people know *that* much about. If the item appeals to a small group of experts, you're already limiting yourself. (Plus, those experts will probably already have bought the item they want with unique specifications—they don't need to trade.) For the rest of the market, perception is everything. If people can't truly perceive the difference in the $500 drone and the $1,000 drone, they'll go for the $500 drone every time.

## "Type A" vs. "Type B" Items

Now that I've traded everything from earrings to margarita glasses to multiple Pelotons to garden tractors, I have a wide frame of reference for making trades. By Trade #4 of the Trade Me Project, I was still figuring this out, but I'd soon discover that every single item falls into one of two categories:

- **TYPE A:** A "Type A" item is one that will appeal to most people. There can be many reasons for this, as I'll cover in future trades, but examples include items that everyone uses or wants (like a computer) or brands that are considered desirable (like a Mustang car).

- **TYPE B:** A "Type B" item is one that requires a specific person to want it. However, that person will value it highly—perhaps even outside its stated dollar value. Examples include a food cart or unicycle. Not everyone is going to want those things, but the person who does want it will *really* want it.

The advantage of Type A items is that your target market is so large. While you'll have to do lots of leg work contacting people and sifting through interest to find your final trade, you don't have to be too strategic about nailing your target demo—because that could be everyone!

On the other hand, while it might take some time and detective work to find your person for a Type B item, they're going to be much more willing to trade with you because they "irrationally" value what you're offering them. Acquiring the item has less to do with function and dollar value and more to do with a specific need or interest they have, which is why becoming an expert on your item and the psychology of your target market is so important.

This is something I'd home in on as I went on trading, but learning to identify whether my item was Type A or Type B would immediately set the stage for my trading strategy.

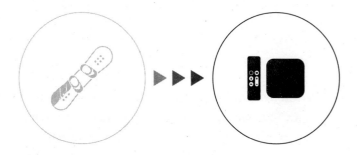

## TRADE 5: SNOWBOARD FOR AN APPLE TV 4K

When I got the snowboard, I took what I'd learned from my vacuum experience and set to work cleaning it up. I used some cleaning products I'd rummaged from under my sink to remove any rust and also sharpened the edges. Then I once again got out my trusty nail polish remover and polished out all the scuffs. It looked awesome by the time I was finished, even though Bobby was still skeptical anyone would want it.

The truth is—I had a solidly Type B item. Not everyone would want a men's snowboard in pretty good condition from 2006, but *someone* would. Most likely a guy who wanted a snowboard but wasn't so into it or so wealthy that he'd be really picky or buy it himself. It had to be a dude who liked snowboarding (or the idea of getting into it) and wasn't trying to buy anything *too* expensive. Now I just had to find him.

---

**Try to identify why someone would want this item to narrow your demographic— and figure out where these people hang out.**

---

I figured the snowboard held about $95 of value based on the comps I had seen on the Internet. I wanted every trade to have ascending value, so I set my filters in the $100–$200 range and started looking for items I wanted. I looked specifically for younger people in San Francisco who seemed like they could be open to trading for a snowboard.

This was way harder than I originally thought it would be. Facebook doesn't let you sort on characteristics like "Seller's Interest in Winter Sports." Anyone I offered the snowboard to came back with an immediate "No." It was too weird to offer people a snowboard—*Why would I need that?!?*— so I needed a new strategy.

I also tried an experiment with Instagram. At this point, I was starting to get inbound Instagram DMs from people who were interested in the item. This should have been great, but it wasn't. There were two problems: 1) Most people weren't interested in trading—they just wanted me to respond to them, and 2) the people who were interested lived far away and shipping the giant snowboard didn't seem feasible. (Ah, a foreshadowing of things to come.)

What if instead of approaching people with my snowboard and hoping I was in my target demo, I brought my target demographic to me? I decided to list the snowboard. I put it on Nextdoor (to keep it local) and Facebook Marketplace for $20, which seemed like an attractive price point. Immediately, I began getting messages.

*Hey, I'm interested in your snowboard,* this one guy wrote me.

*Nice, but I actually don't want money for it,* I wrote back.

Here was the moment of truth.

*Do you have anything you can trade me instead?*

The universal "typing" symbol of a flashing ellipsis popped up. My new buddy was thinking about it. I had a little bit of an advantage in that this was the middle of the COVID-19 pandemic and outdoor rec gear was in high demand and short supply. This gave me a leg up.

*Alright,* he responded, *so my roommate and I both have Apple TVs and we really only need one. Would you take that?*

*What kind of Apple TV?* I asked. *Does it work?*

*A 4K. It's barely used,* he told me.

*Done,* I said.

We arranged for me to drop off the snowboard at his apartment, which was biking distance from where we lived. Bobby strapped the snowboard on his back, and we biked over to the guy's place. He was waiting to meet us, Apple TV 4K in hand.

We made the trade, which Bobby videoed from a distance. I was *elated.*

For the first time, I had traded for something of real value. All the other stuff in the prior trades had been cool, but they were still items I could have found at a garage sale. I had started with a bobby pin, and now I had something I actually wanted and would have spent money on. An Apple TV 4K sold for about $200 new and I'd spent no money getting one. Look how far my bobby pin had come.

For the first time, as I held the Apple TV in my hands, I thought: *I can do this. I'm going to get that house.*

# CHAPTER 4

# TRADE ME PROJECT: BEST BUY EDITION

The problem with the early trades of the Project going so smoothly and picking up momentum with the Apple 4K is I started to believe I'd get to my final goal—trading for a house—pretty quickly.

*Why doesn't everyone do this?* I wondered. It was so easy!

In my next few trades, I found out. Trading, especially trading with an ambitious end goal in mind, is possible, but it's a lot of hard work, requires good strategy, and isn't for the faint of heart. A lot could go wrong—in ways I never would've or could've anticipated.

## TRADE 6: APPLE TV 4K FOR BOSE HEADPHONES

I went into my next trade with enthusiasm. My new Apple TV 4K was definitely a Type A item: Almost everyone could use one and would like to have it—and it had the additional lift of being manufactured by a recognizable and desirable brand. Everyone knows what Apple is. In addition, Apple products are perceived as being luxury and reliable. I was going to have no problem trading this thing away.

---

**Items from credible and desirable brands are easier to trade.**

---

## Let Brands Do the Marketing for You

When items have an identifiable brand, like Apple, Nike, Dyson, etc., those brands will do the hard work for you. Half the battle of trading is getting someone else to see the value of your item. By having a recognizable brand name, people are more likely to want to trade for the item because they recognize the value the item has right off the bat. It's easy to do an Internet search for the make and model of an Apple TV 4K and understand the monetary value; the market already exists, even for used Apple TV 4Ks.

Having that dollar value already in mind gives people a starting point for how to think about the value to them. Something I'd learn later is that certain brands also have their own fan following that makes them also easier to trade. (Just wait until we get into all the car trades later—and I discover the power of a Mustang!) While items that don't have immediate brand recognition are still absolutely "tradable," it will take someone a bit of time to understand if the item is "worth it" instead of knowing off the bat.

I wanted to stay in electronics. Electronics were small, so they were easy to transport, and they tended to retain their value if they were a recent enough model in good shape. Also, San Francisco was the perfect place to be making trades for different electronics, I thought. The supply was massive. Everyone had multiple computers (personal, work, and gaming) and was constantly upgrading for the new iPhone, new headphones, or new gaming console.

I saw myself making easy trades of gradually increasing value, rocketing me toward that house. Proving myself right, it was only a couple days before I identified my next trade: the Apple TV for a nice pair of wireless, noise-cancelling Bose headphones in their original case.

The trade was easy to arrange. I reached out to a guy who was selling his Bose headphones and offered my Apple TV. He liked the deal, and we arranged to meet in the parking lot of a bar near my house. It all seemed so easy. Little did I know that this was and still is probably the strangest trade I've made to date.

At first, it went well. I rolled up on my bike, and the guy was waiting. I pulled out the Apple TV, and he pulled out his headphones. By this time, I'd learned from my past ignorance, so I checked the headphones over quickly to make sure they worked and everything was there. Upon my review, I noticed the charger for the headphones was missing.

Without the charger, the headphones would be useless. I'd messaged him a few hours before to remind him about the accessories, so it was definitely strange he'd forgotten the charger. Either way, the guy—who'd been normal up to that point—got *very* flustered.

"Sorry," I said. "The trade is off unless you have the charger."

"I can go get it," he said.

I was fine with that. Once I commit to a trade, I really want to see it through. I was already over the Apple TV and ready to move on to whatever I could do with the headphones. We could meet later. No big deal.

Then things got weird.

"Can I add you on Find My Friends?" he asked.

For those not familiar, Find My Friends is a feature on your iPhone. If you turn it on for someone, you're automatically and always sharing your location with that person.

"Um, no." I didn't even need to think about it. All the red flags were raised. I barely wanted my best friends knowing my exact location 100% of the time, let alone a guy I didn't know at all.

"Fine," he was getting more frustrated. "I'll just meet up with you later then."

He threw the headphones into his backpack and went storming off. Then, only because Bobby was filming and I double-checked the audio later, I heard him yell *"FUCK."*

You can see my reaction on the video. I turn around, make eye contact with Bobby, and give a nervous shrug. *Never seeing that guy again*, I thought.

But then 30 minutes later, I got a message:

*Got the charger. Meet in 30 at the same place?*

*Sure*, I agreed, because when I want to make a trade, I *really* want to make a trade.

Once again, Bobby and I biked over to the parking lot next to our local bar. The guy was waiting. I gave him the Apple TV and he handed over the headphones, charger included. Then we went our separate ways. So many questions.

To this day, I've no idea if that guy just forgot or if he was trying to scam me and got caught. Either way, it definitely turned my radar on to the fact that trading requires a lot of trust. I needed to be careful about who I was talking to and especially who I was meeting up with. The Trade Me Project has taught me over and over again the power of trusting people you only know over Facebook who'll do awesome things to help out a stranger, but it's also taught me to be careful. Scammers are out there.

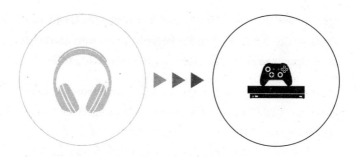

## TRADE 7: BOSE HEADPHONES FOR AN XBOX ONE

My next trade happened shortly thereafter. I'd already found my next item: a new Xbox One with two controllers, two games, and a Kinect Sensor Bar. It took a week or two, but the guy I reached out to with the gaming system agreed to a trade. I met him on the steps of his apartment, and he handed over two bags filled with various Xbox pieces. I checked every piece twice—it was all there. I could barely fit everything in my backpack.

When I got home that night, I made a new video. It showed the headphones and the Xbox trade—and promised greater things to come. This time, though, it wasn't just a video of the objects in my apartment. Like I said, Bobby had taken some footage of me making the trades from afar, like Trade Me Project TMZ footage.

This was the first time I'd appeared on a video as anything other than a disembodied voice. I was nervous about being on camera for reasons varying from safety to just not being super comfortable. Even though I was technically in frame,

I still wasn't really featuring myself in the videos—Bobby had filmed from far away. But I'd been getting more and more comments and messages essentially saying, *Who are you?!?*

In fact, I'd gotten *tons* of messages and comments in general. So many I couldn't even attempt to keep up, but I loved watching them pour in. From the activity feed, I could see just how much action my videos were getting. I could see all the likes, comments, and shares, but most interestingly, I could see people weren't just liking, commenting, and sharing the latest video. Instead, people were seeing a video on their For You page, and instead of just liking and leaving, they were going back to the beginning and watching each of the videos in order, like episodes of their favorite TV show.

It was almost a blessing that I barely had a grasp on the scale of what was happening. I knew people were excited, which added some pressure but also made the whole thing so much more fun. I was energized by the collective interest in and commitment to the Trade Me Project, but I didn't think about it much beyond that. If I had, it might have gotten to my head. Instead, I just focused on making my next trade.

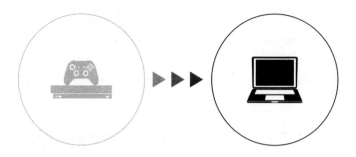

## **TRADE 8:** XBOX ONE FOR A MACBOOK PRO ...

… which was for another medium-value electronic good. It took me about a week, but I found someone in the city who had an extra MacBook Pro. Again, it isn't too weird in San Francisco for people to have extra computers. Usually, your work will hook you up with at least one. Then it's conceivable you might have one for personal use that just sits around.

I was starting to get worried about the difficulty of making future trades. While each trade had pushed me slightly higher in value, I wasn't making the kind of exponential progress I'd been making earlier in the Project. Some of these moves felt almost lateral.

Trading for name-brand items had seemed like an amazing idea in the beginning. People would immediately understand the value and want what I was offering. But there was a downside I hadn't anticipated. There was an organized secondary market for each of these items. In less technical terms, if you wanted a used 2020 Xbox One, it was easy to go online and see all your options. You could quickly get a sense of the price—or if you wanted to sell one, price your own. There was less ability for me to arbitrage with trading and go a step up in value because people always knew what their item was worth and could pretty easily get that amount for it.

---

## The downside of name-brand items is people know their monetary value.

---

This is how I ended up trading for a 2011 MacBook Pro with a guy on Nextdoor. On the day I was supposed to make my trade, I talked a friend of mine into walking with me to go get it (safety in numbers). Unfortunately, we were meeting the guy at a Safeway at the top of literally the steepest hill in San Francisco. We lugged the Xbox up, taking turns carrying it. Then we were given the oldest, heaviest MacBook Pro I'd seen in years. At least the walk was downhill on the way home.

I started offering people in San Francisco my 2011 MacBook Pro. In retrospect, it's predictable no one wanted it. Why would anyone want an old computer if they had the newest model? Plus another slightly newer model too? But I was so disappointed. Was I going to be stuck making fairly lateral trades in low-level electronics forever? I was impatient to make progress toward getting that house.

One of the keys of trading is getting unblocked. If you try trading, sooner or later you'll get stuck. In the beginning, if you're trading low-value items, things shouldn't be too hard, but as you go up in value, it gets trickier. Interestingly, at the highest dollar level, your options start to open up again because value works differently for big-ticket items. In other words, the dollar value of a big-ticket item might not dictate how much someone wants it. You have a little more flexibility and bargaining power.

But those medium-value trades in the $500 to thousands of dollars range can be killers. People are still pretty focused on dollar value and also aren't that flexible about what items they do or don't want. It's easy for them to Google what dollar amount they should be getting for their old iPhone or year-old drone and then stick to that. You have to get creative if you want to break out of mid-level trades and get into the more interesting stuff.

I tried trading away that MacBook Pro in San Francisco for about a week before I realized I needed to switch up my tactics. I wasn't getting strong responses, and I needed to do something different. Up until then, all eight of my trades had taken me just two weeks to complete. Now I'd just spent a whole week on this one stupid computer.

Thinking about it critically, I started to consider what factors I could change in my approach. That's when I realized that while the electronics market is saturated in San Francisco, that wasn't true of other places. In fact, I'd noticed tons of comments from viewers in other places saying how much they wanted the computer. So I got on my accounts and reset the geographic range of my search.

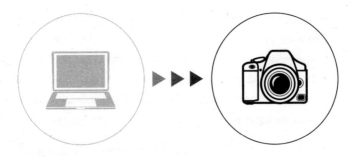

## TRADE 9: MACBOOK PRO FOR A CANON CAMERA

I found my next trade on my old friend, Facebook Marketplace. As I'd predicted, as soon as I started looking outside San Francisco, I got tons of interest right away. Whether it was for school or work or just personal use, lots of people wanted a 2011 MacBook Pro.

Changing your geographic focus can be a smart way to unblock yourself, as not every market is the same. You can make some guesses about the characteristics of each local market that can hinder or help your trade. For example, if you want to trade for skis, setting your location to mountain ski towns is a great move. Theoretically, people will have lots of extra sets of skis to trade away. But if you're looking to trade for a jet ski, then you don't want to look in ski towns; you want to go right to Florida or the Great Lakes.

Sometimes, regionality isn't a specific city. For example, if I'm looking for a tractor, I'd look in agricultural areas. I can trade for and trade away a tractor much more easily in those markets. It isn't just about supply but also demand. What do people in this specific market want? No one needs a boat in Palm Springs, but boats are really popular in Michigan.

---

## One method for getting unblocked is to change up your geographic region.

---

In this case, scarcity really helped me out. Computers were oversupplied in San Francisco but undersupplied elsewhere. This is how I found Caitriona. She lives in Wisconsin. We met in my Instagram DMs, the first inbound interest I got that converted into a trade. She offered me a really nice Canon camera with a few different lenses. I was intrigued. The camera was still in the electronics category, but it would at least help me get rid of this seemingly ancient MacBook Pro.

Caitriona was open to trading and wanted the MacBook Pro. However, the whole idea of just sending off her expensive camera in the mail and hoping a computer arrived from a totally random Internet stranger was too much for her. She was extremely spooked.

*How does this work exactly?* she messaged me.

I understood and was sympathetic to her concerns. I knew my intentions were good, but she had no reason to trust me. What guarantee did she have that this wasn't a giant scam?

I started sending her DMs with lots of photos of the computer to show her exactly what kind of shape it was in.

I was friendly and responsive. For the first time, I truly had to get into the mindset of my trade partner and anticipate what her objections would be.

---

### Understanding the psychology of the person on the other end of the trade is critical.

---

As we chatted, I could tell she was getting more comfortable. She just needed a better sense of me and a complete understanding of how trading would work. I explained the entire process, including how we'd handle shipping and what expectations were in terms of timing.

I also flipped it back on her, asking her lots of questions about her camera. The irony here is I've never taken a photography class, and at that time, I knew almost nothing about cameras, as my early Trade Me Project videos showed.

*I'll have the shutter count later,* she messaged me at one point in response to something I'd asked her.

I remember thinking, *What does that even mean?* But I pretended like I knew exactly what she was saying. Challenging the other person to explain or defend their item weirdly has the effect of making them more interested in the trade, I'd discover. In this case, I was mostly just trying to figure out what I was getting as part of the package, but having her explain her camera and its accessories helped engage her in the process.

Getting her to the point where she'd put her camera in the mail was huge. She was in, but she was still worried. Finally, after days of chatting, I decided to end the standoff.

*I mailed the computer to you today,* I DMed her.

Then I sent a screenshot of the receipt with the tracking number. I'd done it. It was one of the few levers I could pull.

## Understand Your Levers

When you make a trade, it isn't as simple as exchanging an item one for one. There are other ways to influence the person you're trading with to make the trade seem more enticing. I call these your levers. Levers are critical in trading because you can't throw in cash to sweeten a deal, so you have to find other ways to get the other person to a "Yes." Whenever I approach a trade, beyond the basics of making sure I have a strong item and I'm targeting the right people, I'm always thinking about what other levers I can pull to close the trade. Handling shipping and logistics is often the most important one—there's real value in taking an unwanted item off someone's hands and replacing it with something they do want, all with little effort on their part—but you'll learn others over the course of this book. Keep in mind that one of the levers of the Trade Me Project would end up being the platform the Project gained from its popularity. This isn't a lever everyone can pull, but it would end up being important to several trades in the Project.

I'd come to learn that as soon as the other person agreed to the trade, I should get my item in the mail right away. This bound them to the trade and limited the time they had to panic and back out. (Of course, I always run the risk that someone not only backs out but also refuses to send their item, but this hasn't happened to me—yet.)

## Don't give people time to back out.

Finally, that magic message came through.

*Me too.*

That was it! Now all I could do was wait and hope.

## CHAPTER 5

# WHEREIN I BECOME A SNEAKERHEAD

Waiting and hoping would become a theme when it came to mailing trade items for the Trade Me Project. Putting anything in the mail became a real gamble during the COVID-19 pandemic. Shipping times were 10 times longer than they had been. The delays were understandable, but that didn't make them any less nerve-wracking.

When the package from Caitriona showed up about a week later, I was thrilled. I filmed an unboxing—in true millennial style—as part of the TikTok video covering the trade. In the video, I say this was my first time mailing a trade, but that wasn't exactly true. My very first trade exchanging my bobby pins for earrings had also been mailed across the country, but I was scarred by how long that took and had been trying to keep all my trades local ever since.

If you watch my videos sequentially, you'll notice that the quality starts to get much better around this point in the Trade Me Project. This is because I finally got some help. With almost no production experience, I'd been scripting, filming, editing, and uploading all my videos myself. I was sort of embarrassed to be on camera, so I'd often go hide in a corner of our apartment when I needed to film.

Looking at my content, I decided live footage of the trades would be a cool add in the videos. Bobby saw how much time was going toward creating and editing content, so he asked if he could help. If I did the trades and he focused on video production, we could get much more done. Little did I know, he actually had tons of experience creating digital video and was amazing at it.

As soon as Bobby took over the video production side of the Project, the quality went up dramatically. He was creative about editing and introduced interesting effects. He also had novel concepts, like taking B-roll footage to help set the stage and tell the story. My videos went from my filming my computer screen to creating mini productions. It was fun to discover this skill set I didn't know he had. The Trade Me Project went from something I was obsessively doing on my own to a cool thing we were able to work on together.

Bobby taking over the video side freed me up to totally focus on trading. Sending out messages and scrolling through listings was taking up more and more of my day. While I was still only available outside traditional work hours, it was incredible how all-consuming the Project became.

I was still unsure about engaging with my followers on TikTok. The volume was way too much for me to respond to people personally, but I started to break the ice a little on my Internet anonymity.

For example, when I hit 3 million followers, I recorded my first nontrading video that fully showed me. At the time, there was a trend where people would create shapes out of pasta on flattened cardboard. Then they'd film themselves using the cardboard panel to launch the pasta into the air. If you slowed down the frames, viewers could see the shape the pasta was making in the air for a split second before it all came raining down. I copied the challenge.

*Thanks for* … I wrote at the top of the video—and then tossed *3M* in pasta in the air.

Next, I added the phrase I'd been saying since the beginning, also in pasta:

*LET'S*

*GET*

*THAT*

*(and the shape of a house).*

Then I teased my next trade—coming Monday.

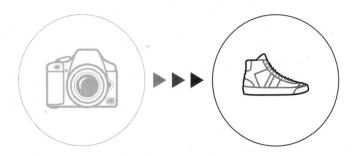

## TRADE 11: CANON CAMERA FOR OFF-WHITE NIKE BLAZERS

I was done with electronics. I'd successfully made four electronics trades in a row, and the camera had been a potentially precarious move. I lacked experience in DSLRs, and while I was able to quickly learn about the market, I was worried that not understanding the specific values of lenses and their setups could make it hard to make a good trade.

Luckily, Caitriona's Canon camera was nice, and the lenses it came with were expensive. People who were in this price range had a particular idea of the setup they wanted and were willing to spend money to get *exactly* what they wanted. Tracking down my next trade only took another week, but it felt like forever. For a moment, I was worried I'd spend the rest of my life making electronics trades of incrementally better value.

Carrying that energy into my next trade, my thinking was: the further from electronics the better. If I was outside my area of expertise with cameras, I was about to leave my comfort zone way behind.

My next trade partner, Scott, found me over Instagram. He reached out to me in my DMs.

*Hey I have a valuable item I'd like to trade you,* he wrote. *It's a slightly used pair of off white x nike sneakers.*

The sneakers in question were, specifically, Nike Blazer Mid Off-White All Hallows Eve. They were a pale orange color with a bright orange swoop. Released in 2018, they had been super popular ever since. They were even one of the pairs Billie Eilish selected in the Complex's famous "Sneaker Shopping" YouTube series.

I had *zero* idea how big the world of sneakers is and how seriously sneakerheads take their collections. Scott and I haggled back and forth. The sneakers were listed at $888 (random), but they didn't look like they were in amazing shape. He insisted this was just bad lighting, so I asked for better-lit photos. I still wasn't sold on the condition and suggested he take a video. Appearing skeptical in the beginning made him more eager to sell it.

Eventually, I agreed. Once I was in, I pushed the process, immediately putting the camera in the mail and sending him the tracking information.

But before I could launch my nascent sneakerhead career, tragedy struck. I'd mailed a few trades so far without a problem. Waiting always made me anxious, but everything eventually arrived at my apartment in good condition.

Until this time.

About a week into waiting for the sneakers to get dropped off by UPS, I started to get nervous. I checked the tracking number—no movement. This was extremely not good. I started making calls, and UPS said the package wasn't stuck somewhere—it was just straight up missing. I called UPS and tried to put a stop on the camera, but it was already on its way. I gave Scott a heads-up, and he was immediately suspicious.

*How do I know you're being honest tho?*

He went on to insinuate I hadn't actually sent the camera and was just pretending the shoes had never come. I got it, but it was easy enough to have him call UPS and verify. Thus began the saga of the missing shoes.

I wasn't so lucky on my end. The shoes had vanished. I called UPS almost every day, but no one could locate the shoes. Finally, after a few calls, I got someone on the phone at the centralized UPS location in San Francisco, where I knew the package must be. After pinpointing their location based on when the shoes had been sent and when they went missing, I knew I had to go get this person to go look for the shoes. So I told them these were my wedding shoes, and my wedding was happening this weekend.

(I'm not going to advise you to lie, but in this case …)

It worked. The guy found the shoes and put them on the truck to be delivered that day.

My relief when I unboxed the Blazers was palpable. I had so many people watching me at this point that getting derailed by a shipping issue would have been awful.

I wish I had a better takeaway from this experience than "Sometimes, things get lost in the mail," but it's true. Sometimes, even though you use a fancy service and pay for tracking, stuff just goes missing in the mail. Make sure you get insurance—although in this case, even if I'd recovered the value, I still would've been starting over. So do what you have to do to track down missing items, even if it means getting creative and going the extra mile.

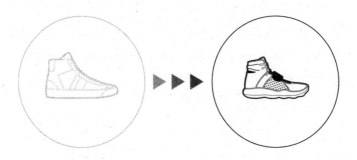

## TRADE 10: OFF-WHITE BLAZERS FOR OFF-WHITE HYPERDUNKS

Now that I was in Sneaker World, I didn't want to leave. I'd discovered something fascinating. Up to this point, the hundreds—maybe even thousands—of people I'd reached out to had been weirded out by trading, but sneakerheads weren't. In fact, trading was a common practice in the sneakerhead community. This made my life so, so much easier.

---

### Leverage existing barter networks.

---

There aren't many existing barter networks in North America. As I've observed, people in the States really prefer to use money as a medium of exchange. However, barter networks do exist. Some are set up around sustainability principles, and some are just about the mechanism of trading (i.e., people in the network just enjoy bartering goods and services). Others are focused on a particular type of item that inspires a community of fans.

Often, these items are collectibles. My theory is that even though collectibles might have a set dollar value, their "real" value fluctuates based on each individual collector's preferences. For example, a certain Pokemon card might be worth $500 on the open market (of eBay), but one collector will value it in particular because it fits their collection's theme or is one of the few cards they're missing. Same goes for art or rare books or Hummel figurines or stamps or any number of things. It was definitely true of sneakers.

While my Blazers had a certain value based on what they were selling for on sites like GOAT, StockX, or eBay, that didn't mean someone would only trade me another pair of sneakers of equal value for them. If someone really wanted this pair because this was the particular kind of shoe they collected, they might offer me a pair that was even more valuable on the open market. This is exactly what happened.

## Leveraging Existing Barter Markets

Some items have existing barter markets that already exist or at least a demographic of people that would be open to making a trade or have made trades in the past. Sneakers are a great example of this, as trading in the sneakerhead community is commonplace; surfboards are another example (not that I've tried trading these). In leveraging these existing networks, you bypass one of the hurdles when trying to make a trade, which is getting someone to agree to trading versus exchanging value via money. I've been able to talk a lot of people into trading, but you'd be surprised how accustomed people are to using money and how resistant people are to thinking about value outside of money. If trading itself isn't a barrier, the trade becomes about matching the person with the right item instead of having to convince them a trade is a valuable way to get something they want. Good luck finding these communities! Barter systems are more common outside the United States, but I don't come across them as often as I wish I did.

I didn't mean to keep making sneaker trades, but it was just so easy. I even used the metaphor "shooting fish in a barrel" at one point to describe my experience. Sneakerheads are a true community who've found each other on certain digital platforms. For example, most sneakerheads have Instagram accounts where they show off their collections. They follow each other and use their social media accounts to list sneakers for sale or trade.

Once I caught wind of this, it was incredible. All I had to do was search for sneaker accounts on Instagram and then look at who was following those accounts. I could keep digging deeper and deeper. My target demographic was literally sitting in front of me, and I knew exactly what they wanted. They'd organized themselves for me into a thriving digital micro-market.

I began to notice that people got *hyper*-specific about what they collected. Sure, some people just bought the most expensive shoes (not that I knew what those were), but most people seemed to have a real focus. Cluing into that, I started searching for fan groups of the brand of shoes I had.

On Facebook and Instagram, I began joining groups with names like "Nike Off-White Sneakers Anonymous SF."

Getting into these groups proved to be a super effective way of directly connecting with my target demo. The whole part of trading where I had to hope the person on the other end would want what I was offering felt totally solved, as I knew for sure the Facebook group had only people interested in one particular brand of shoes—exactly what I was offering.

---

## Go straight to your customer by finding digital fan groups.

---

Once I realized these groups existed, I started joining them like crazy. Since then, social media groups have become one of my most useful ways to connect and make trades. I rely on them constantly now, and I'm part of Internet communities all over the world.

I mean it. Here are examples of Facebook groups I currently belong to:

- Park Slope housing *(I've never lived in Park Slope)*

- See the USA via road trips *(didn't do that)*

- Americans living in Denmark *(accurate for one summer)*

- I'm getting married in Western Michigan *(I didn't)*

- Support Napa Valley restaurants *(a noble cause)*

- Animal travelers *(My dog, Earl, deserves an entire book just on him.)*

- Visit Mexico City *(never been)*

  They get more strange:

- Expecting moms of New York *(not relevant to me)*

- New York images from 1850-1980 *(extremely not relevant to me)*

- Ohio State University sublets *(I've no idea why I joined this)*

Facebook and Instagram groups have become such a key element of the Trade Me Project that I almost forget what it was like not to be using them obsessively. Discovering them during this series of trades was so important. It was in one of these groups that I found my next trade.

Within one of the Off-White fan groups, I met Jonny, a guy who was really interested in my Blazers. We quickly moved our convo to Instagram DMs.

I was once again reluctant. While I'd gotten excited by the sneaker market, did I really want to get stuck in shoes? I'd just gone on a long run of electronics—and it was kind of a pain.

But Jonny was persistent. He kept messaging me different options. Eventually, he offered me a pair of Nike Off-White Hyperdunks, which kind of look like what you'd wear to play basketball in space. I looked up the value of the shoes and they historically sold for more than what my Blazers did ($800+). To me, all these shoes were just dollar signs, so I didn't understand taking a hit in value. It was so cut and dry—why give someone $900 shoes for $850 shoes? But for a real collector, the dollar value didn't matter. He just really wanted this specific pair of shoes.

Actually, at first, it did matter. He asked if I'd sweeten the deal by throwing in $50 to make it more fair.

*I really gotta do a 1:1*, I told him. *Just clean trades.*

He told me that was fine, but in that case, he'd keep the box and laces.

*Ah ok I'm actually gonna pass. I was hoping for the box. Thanks so much though.*

*Haha alright,* he responded. *I can include the box but I'm gonna keep the laces if that's cool.*

I didn't get it, but I respected it. We agreed to trade and made a plan to meet up later that night in the parking lot of a local Whole Foods.

In the TikTok video, you'll see me biking in the freezing cold fully masked up, as we had to be in the summer of 2020. Jonny checked out my sneakers and proclaimed them solid, then handed over his pair. Looked like it was all there to me, minus the laces.

Awesome.

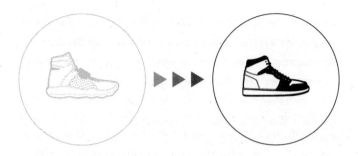

## TRADE 12: NIKE OFF-WHITE HYPERDUNKS FOR JORDAN 1 SHATTERED BACKBOARDS

After Jonny and I made the trade, I featured his account, @theworkssf, on my Instagram and left a referral. I was learning that's how it worked in the sneaker game. You kind of establish your credibility by trading with other people in the community and building a reputation.

I was having such good luck, so why not continue? I went back to my Facebook and Instagram groups to share my new sneakers. I also started messaging people who followed sneaker accounts and then messaging those people's friends and then their friends' friends—and I got hit with a rate limit.

This isn't like being banned. All it means is if you send the same (or similar) message to too many people over a short period of time, Instagram stops you from sending more messages—sometimes for a few hours and sometimes for a few days.

While I waited for my rate limit to expire, I logged into my personal Instagram account and started researching potential trade partners and sending messages. And I got hit with much more scrutiny.

Here's the thing: As my own self, I didn't have any cred in these groups. I wasn't a long-time sneakerhead who was established in the network—and I no longer had a little blue check mark to make up for my lack of history. I didn't realize how valuable verification was until it was gone.

## The Value of Verification

Being verified on a social media platform means the platform—whether Twitter (where verification started), Instagram, or TikTok—has proven that you are who you say you are. Not only does verification mean you're real, but it also gives you credibility. Celebrities or important brands are offered verification proactively, but the rest of us can apply for it. It might take a few rounds of applications and a certain number of followers for the social media platform to agree to verify you.

I'd been verified on TikTok fairly quickly—within the first month of trading—and I'd just requested Instagram do the same without really thinking about it. I immediately got verified, which seemed cool but wasn't especially useful. (My guess about why my request was approved is there weren't many TikTokers at that time who were also crossing over onto Instagram.)

No one wants to get scammed. We all know what Twitter bots and weird phishing emails look like. There wasn't anything about my personal profile that raised red flags—my username wasn't @ubcdr7343854676, for example—but it didn't matter. Without my little blue check mark, no one trusted me. I looked just like the scammers I was so desperate to avoid.

## Managing Trade Accounts

To this day, I find myself rate-limited or straight up blocked on Instagram and Facebook every couple months depending on how hard I'm looking for a trade at the time. While I wouldn't suggest multiple accounts, I will say I have them to use as backups when an account gets blocked.

The problem with having multiple accounts is that you need to remember who you've reached out to. I've had situations where someone replies and says, *Someone else just messaged me and asked me to trade for their skateboard.* This immediately makes people feel like it's a scam. Little do they know it's the same person on the other end who had their original account rate-limited.

Even reaching out from my verified account, I'd sent *so* many messages by this time that people in the local sneaker community were starting to get sketched out too. I began seeing my name and account handles popping up as a topic of discussion in the various groups as people speculated about whether I was real or not. One kid—an actual child— challenged me to immediately post a video on TikTok to prove I was real.

I messaged my buddy Jonny again, explaining the situation.

Unlike me, he had an established reputation in the sneakerhead circles. With just one Insta story, he explained who I was and said I could be trusted. He also told me not to worry: Most of these people were middle schoolers and high schoolers—and it was a tough group to be in unless you knew the right people. I was back in business.

My goal with this trade was to get past the $1,000 mark with the new shoes, ideally for something that wasn't shoes. But most sneakerheads only had shoes available to trade, so I was kind of stuck. Also, now *I* was paranoid about getting scammed. So when I found something I thought looked good, I sent it to Jonny.

*Tbh they look kind of sus to me,* he responded. *I don't like the way the heel logo looks.*

That's how I passed on a nice—but very undervalued—pair of Travis Scott Jordans, which is great because, as Jonny told me, there were a lot of fakes of those on the market.

Having Jonny as a resource was amazing. I'd already rolled the dice with my lack of domain expertise with the camera, so did I really want to risk things again with sneakers? I could read about how to identify fakes or what the best sneakers to trade for were, but why? Instead, I called on an expert who was knowledgeable and generous.

---

## Don't be afraid to phone an expert friend.

---

I even started to try to authenticate the sneakers on my own using services like CheckCheck, but Jonny warned me that wasn't foolproof. People could send you screenshots of shoes that weren't theirs and then scam you with fakes.

(Just a side note: I spent $2 getting those shoes verified on CheckCheck and felt guilty for days. I'd spent money—did this ruin the integrity of the Project?!? This shows you how seriously I was taking my self-imposed rules.)

Then I sent Jonny a photo of a pair of shoes that—

*Yeah those were mine*, he messaged me. *That's my blue blanket.*

Apparently, he had traded this exact pair to the guy I was now messaging with. He recognized the shoes—the guy had reused the photos Jonny had sent him. I ended up passing on the trade, but it was crazy to see how connected the sneaker world was in San Francisco.

Again, I wasn't a sneakerhead myself, but having help from someone who was passionate about the stuff I was looking at was huge. He helped me navigate through thousands of listings of what just looked like colorful, weird-shaped shoes to me until I also started to learn the market.

Finally, Jonny signed off on a trade: a pair of Jordan 1 Shattered Backboards (no idea; they're white and orange), which were owned by some teenagers. Was it ethical to trade with teenagers?

I wish I could say the Trade Me Project was powered by trading with entrepreneurial teens who got really creative, but that isn't true. In fact, the few times I've had an item that teens really want, the response is fun but not exactly a great use of time. I get thousands of inbound messages from preteens asking if I'll trade with them.

This goes one of two ways: 1) They aren't actually interested in trading—they just want me to respond, or 2) they do want to trade, but they can't because they're 13 and don't own anything of value.

*Amazing.*

But these teens were real, and I wanted their shoes. Sneakers—sorry.

I sent Jonny a few more photos, showing all the angles and their commentary.

*I would definitely do it*, Jonny wrote me.

I met the teens on a sidewalk in San Francisco, and we made our trade.

If you've watched the video, you can see that on the content side, we were really starting to figure out what people found interesting. Gone were the long intros where I recounted every single trade before getting to the point. Gone was the shaky camera work. Gone was the fuzzy, disembodied voice. I was in front of the camera, we had great action shots, and I was figuring out how to set up the cadence of the videos so each one would end with a little teaser for the next trade.

Telling that story and getting people hooked has been so important in building our audience. The videos couldn't be too long, but they had to set the stage. People needed just enough information that if they were watching me for the first time, they understood what was going on. But there couldn't be so much context that my legacy followers got annoyed. *Stop saying all your trades every time*, about 6,000 people had written on my previous videos. Feedback received.

Featuring my trading partners in my videos was tricky. I learned the hard way I needed to ask their permission. Because I was so unaware of how big my platform was for the longest time, I didn't even think about it. When I traded for the 2011 MacBook Pro, I put up footage of me and the guy making the swap. He messaged me almost right away, totally freaked out I had shared his image with millions of people.

I felt terrible. He was totally right, and I should have asked. I immediately took down the video, blurred his face, and reuploaded it. For every subsequent trade, I made sure to ask permission before showing anyone's face. Most people had no problem with it. In fact, I'd discover that giving someone fleeting TikTok fame ended up being a valuable lever I could pull to sweeten the deal when I was trying to push a trade.

This was definitely true of the guys who'd traded with me for the Shattered Backboards. They were hyped on the idea of being featured on a TikTok account that guaranteed at least 3 million people would see their own social media accounts, which they'd then use to raise their profile and make more trades or sales.

Say what you will about Gen Z, but they know the value of good publicity. It was the first time my trading partners had understood the added value of my platform because sneakerheads already did this for each other when they traded.

I wouldn't forget it.

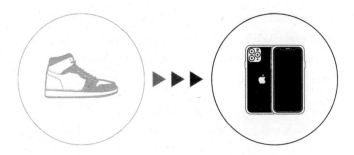

## TRADE 13: JORDAN 1 SHATTERED BACKBOARDS FOR AN IPHONE 11 PRO MAX

I knew I had to get out of the sneaker game. I'd fallen into it, gotten obsessed, learned everything I could, done some great trades, and made some good friends. But it was time to say goodbye and move on to the next great thing.

This is kind of how it goes for me. I'll get really into an item or a category of items for a while. Then, once I figure it out, I'm ready to move on. This is a crucial part of trading—or at least trading up. You can't get so myopic that you get stuck. You need to be able to look up and see what else is out there.

Fortunately, interest in my Jordan 1s was high. The guy I eventually traded with contacted me. He wanted to just buy them outright.

I had it in my head that I wanted to trade for an Apple iPad or iPhone. The Apple brand had worked wonders for me—if I could make sure I only traded for newer products. I told the guy I wouldn't take money from him, but he could go trade—or whatever—with someone who had new, lightly used Apple products. Ideally, an iPhone was what I was after. I even sent him a listing for one.

*So if I get this phone you will trade me for the shoes.*

I could practically hear his confusion (*skepticism? disdain?*).

*That's right*, I told him.

He was game to try, but he needed a lot of coaching. Even though I'd only been trading for about a month, I had no idea how much I'd learned about reaching out to people on all the different platforms and negotiating a deal to make a trade.

Predictably, most of the people he reached out to went dark. That's how it goes. He made a few more attempts and then gave up. He kept offering me money and didn't understand why I was throwing up this weird roadblock. So I did the only thing I could think to do: I found the phone for him.

Sometimes, the only way to get unblocked is to broker a trade. In this case, I brokered a sale. I found a new iPhone 11 Pro Max for sale for under the price he'd offered me for the shoes. Because the sticking point for him had been negotiating and setting up the logistics of the sale with Internet sellers, I took care of all that for him. I negotiated the price, and I arranged the exchange. All he had to do was show up with cash and then come trade me the iPhone.

## Beware the Made-Up Mind

People who already have an endgame in mind for after they sell their item are some of the hardest to trade with. For example, if someone has a jet ski on sale on Facebook Marketplace and immediately lets me know they hope to use the money from that sale to buy a boat, it'll be very hard for me to convince them that instead of selling the jet ski, they should trade for something else (unless the item I'm offering to trade is indeed a boat). Because the person already has an endgame for what they'll use the money for, they'll be nearly impossible to convince that money isn't what they want. On the other hand, if people *really* want the item you have and are even willing to spend money on it, then you have even more bargaining power.

I sent him the address and contact information—and then waited. Was he going to come through? I had no idea, but I knew how badly he wanted these shoes given that he was willing to entertain this whole thing at all. Then he texted me a photo of the iPhone.

The guy showed up at the Ferry building in San Francisco, where we'd arranged to meet, with phone in hand. I propped my phone on my bike to record the trade. Then I handed him the sneakers, which he promptly put on Instagram and sold for even more money (good for him). I also featured him in my social media accounts, as he'd requested.

I felt like a genius brokering that trade. This was a light bulb moment for me. If someone wanted to trade but didn't have an item I wanted, I could help them buy or trade something else. I couldn't sweeten the deal with money, but my willingness to do the work was a value-add—another lever I could pull.

If I thought helping someone buy a used iPhone was crazy, the next few trades were going to prove that in addition to making trades, I was also going to have to be an expert in brokering them.

## CHAPTER 6

# THAT TIME A RED VAN DRIPPED GOO

A minivan fell in my lap. And it was all thanks to the power of the Trade Me Project.

I opened my Instagram one day and found a series of messages from a woman who was a follower and fan of the Trade Me Project. She loved it so much, she wanted to be part of it. She and her husband had just bought a new van, and they didn't need their old one. Did I want it?

Did I want *a car*?

Yes. Yes, I definitely did.

*Where is the van?* I asked her.

*Minnesota,* she told me. *But we can drive it out to you.*

*No. Way.* I thought, *There's no way this is real.*

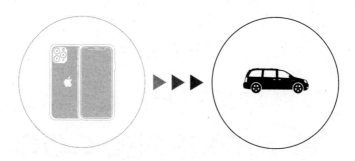

## TRADE 14: IPHONE 11 PRO MAX FOR A 2008 DODGE GRAND CARAVAN

Why would someone offer to trade me a whole van for one iPhone *and* also drive it practically across the country for me at no additional cost?

After hundreds—maybe even thousands—of messages accusing me of being a scammer, I was pretty sure I was being hit with the biggest scam of all time.

Every time I make a trade, I try to think about what the other person is getting out of it. This is part of assessing their psychology. What do they want? How can I make my item more valuable to them? Does it help to be super eager or should I hold back? Getting into someone's head helps me negotiate better to close trades. (I'll talk about this more in my next trade.)

In this case, I couldn't figure out what the woman was getting out of it. The gas money, the cost of sleeping in hotels, the time spent driving across the country. An iPhone—even a new one—didn't offset the value they were offering. I didn't get it.

I considered just walking away from something that was clearly too good to be true, but I thought I could ask a few more questions just to get a clearer picture.

She explained that for her, it wasn't about the items—she just loved the barter economy. Her husband hopped in the chat too. He confirmed what she was saying. They just thought trading was really neat and wanted to be a part of the Trade Me Project, of which they were big fans. This was the first time someone had reached out to make a trade because they were generally interested in what I was doing, not in the item I had. It was still a surprise to me, but I loved their enthusiasm, and this seemed like an amazing next step for the Trade Me Project.

So, we made a deal. They would drive all the way to San Francisco to exchange their van for my iPhone. I couldn't believe that less than two months in, my bobby pin had become a *car*.

Before my trading partners arrived, I began thinking about how I could create publicity for this trade beyond my digital channels. At this point, the Trade Me Project had enough momentum that I was pretty sure I could get traditional news media interested. Also, what would make a better visual than the van coming down the hill in San Francisco?

Bobby and I had been working hard to professionalize our content for TikTok. We even got a drone and filmed some cool footage of me in Dolores Park, showing off a bobby pin (not *the* bobby pin, of course) and explaining the project. Kind of like an intro video recapping my progress so far for people who were new to the project.

As I was waiting for the van to arrive, I even began experimenting with doing live streams and dueting with other TikTokers (when you embed their video and respond to it). Because the trade was in the bag, I had extra time to play around with content. Also, I didn't want to lose anyone's interest. All my trades had been fast so far. Would making people wait a couple weeks mean my audience lost interest? People expected updates on at least a weekly basis. If I was quiet for more than a few days, I got comments asking when the next trade was coming. My filler videos were one way to make sure I kept in touch.

We'd also gotten better at teaser content. After the fancy drone video, I uploaded another one recapping my progress again with footage cut in that the couple had taken for me as they drove. Rolling hills, long grassy plains, and steep mountains. It was clear this was a trek.

*My next trade is on its way here*, I told my followers, *and it's a big one.*

Being able to tell the story of the Trade Me Project this way helped me put together a pitch for local news. I'd gotten some inbound requests as the project gained traction, but I didn't have anything "special" enough to share. Once the van happened, I replied and told them I had a big trade, and they'd want to be there. ABC News agreed to come cover the van's arrival. The Trade Me Project was going national.

When the day in question came, it was so surreal as camera crews set up. I didn't have a parking spot in San Francisco; actually, I didn't even have a car. So we decided they could meet us near my friend Mike's house, as he had a garage.

As the minutes ticked down, I got more nervous. It all felt so crazy. What if after everything, it *was* a scam, and I was finished—on camera?

Then I got a text from my trade partner that they were close. I'll never forget the visual of identical minivans—one of which they were trading; the other they were driving home—rolling down my hill.

Meeting the couple who'd driven all the way from Minnesota was lovely. Their whole family had made the trip, and it was one of their kid's birthdays. Bobby and I had gotten them some treats for the ride home.

Meanwhile, the crews started filming, getting B-roll footage and interviewing all of us. They got some shots of us making the official handoff. I handed over the iPhone, and they gave me the keys and title to the car. Then they drove away. Mission accomplished.

I took a picture of myself on the hood and posted it to Instagram. The photo blew up, and I started getting all kinds of requests from news channels and digital news platforms. In the next few days, I probably did 20 to 30 interviews. I think the idea that I had gone from a tiny bobby pin to an actual car was very exciting for people and made journalists want to reach out.

Many of them wanted to know how long it would take me to get to a house or what the house would look like. I told all of them I didn't know, but I'd get the house eventually—even if it took me 20 years.

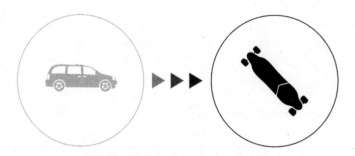

## TRADE 15: 2008 DODGE GRAND CARAVAN FOR A BOOSTED BOARD

After all that fanfare, we came back to check on the car the next morning. I got in the car, put the keys in the ignition, and … it wouldn't start.

The more I looked over the van, the more it became clear that it was in pretty rough shape. It was still an unbelievable trade, and I was so grateful, but this wasn't good. It wasn't that I thought I'd been scammed or tricked. This couple went above and beyond to be awesome participants in the Trade Me Project. I knew I was getting a used car with lots of miles, but something was really off with the van itself.

We were in trouble. San Francisco is very serious about parking. Getting a permit to park in the neighborhoods requires presenting all kinds of documentation that you actually live there, and it's always a fight for spots. We'd managed to move the van to a public parking space before it quit working altogether, but now it was stuck. I had to move it within 48 hours or it would be towed.

How had I gone from surprise vans and national news crews and all the excitement to … this? Trading truly has high highs and low lows.

Later that afternoon, things looked even worse. Bobby and I went to check on the van again—still there (phew!)—and we noticed a puddle of weird stuff under the car. I got down on my hands and knees to check it out, and the van was dripping what looked like goopy red fluid. We inspected it carefully and called some friends who were experts. The issues were almost too numerous to list. A lot of work would need to be done on the van to make it run reliably.

*What had I done?*

I needed to get this van traded—and fast.

After waiting for the van drive all the way from Minnesota, I knew I wanted to do this next trade locally. Even though the van had problems, it looked like a good deal if you were willing to make repairs. I got all kinds of messages from people who had no problem trading for the van.

*Hola. Sigue disponible?* read one Facebook Message I got.

*Hi yes*, I responded, using Google Translate.

*Price 1700*, was the response.

How did I explain in Spanish that I wasn't selling the van, I was trading it?

Instead of trying to explain it, I just sent all the specs for the van and then sent the listing for an ebike I'd found.

*Okay I will trade for this*, I wrote.

Surprisingly, the guy agreed to come look at the car, and we set a time to meet.

He came to inspect it that night, along with a bunch of other people who'd found me via Facebook Marketplace. Almost all of them took one look at my oozing red van and said "No." This guy seemed a little more interested but also concerned. He called up his buddy, who was a mechanic, and explained the issues over the phone. Then he took off.

I sat there alone in the dark. I didn't want to leave the car in the spot overnight because I was sure it'd get towed. Eventually, I sat at a bus stop under a streetlamp just guarding the car. It was so stupid. This might have been the darkest moment of this whole experience.

*I won't get the trade done, the car will get towed, and then it will all be over.*

Just in time for my slot celebrating the Trade Me Project to air on the news, of course.

But all hope wasn't lost.

After the one guy left, he sent me his phone number, and I called. Getting on the phone always helps (if the other person is willing). With our limited language skills, we managed to communicate through the trade. The original "price" we had talked about was too high. His mechanic told him the van would need at least $1,600 worth of repairs, which was a great way to negotiate for a better price. I tried to reset the value at $1,200 so I could then go find an item in that range, but the guy wasn't having it. $1,000 at most.

I was desperate.

I agreed.

Then I started scrambling. I couldn't sell the car, so I went all over the Internet looking at items listed for $1,000 and under. I would've just sent the guy some items I was willing to trade for and let him figure out acquiring them, but I knew that my pool of potential trades was way larger than this guy's, even just based on language skills. I had to help him broker the deal.

Just like with the sneakers and iPhone, trades aren't always directly between two people. If only it were that simple. However, if I hadn't gotten into the business of brokering trades, I'd have never even come close to finishing the Project. If you really want to trade, sometimes you have to get creative.

## Possible Trading Scenarios

- **Option 1:** In the most efficient scenario, the other person wants what I have—and vice versa. We trade with each other directly.

- **Option 2:** I want what the other person has, but they don't want what I have. So I have to trade my item for something they want to make the original trade.

- **Option 3:** The other person wants what I have, but I don't want what they have, so they need to go trade for or buy something else.

- **Option 4:** Both of us could trade our original items for things the other person wants, but this is so complicated that it's likely a nonstarter.

Option 1 is obviously the best and most simple scenario, but it happens less often than I'd like. If you're really committed to trading, you're quickly going to find yourself in the other scenarios.

If I have to get creative, I prefer Option 2. Option 2 doesn't require extra effort from the other person. All they have to do is wait while I go figure out an intermediary trade. Then I come to them with the item they want.

Option 3 works too, but it takes a little more effort. Getting the other person to cooperate in tracking down another item can be tough. The best way to move along the process is to help as much as you can. You want to remove those barriers for people. So if you do the work of finding their trade for them and setting it up so all they have to do is show up, they're more likely to participate. Doing the work for them is an excellent lever you can pull.

---

### If you need to broker a trade for your trade partner, offer to do the work.

---

This is exactly what I did for the man who wanted the van (who was using the handle @Iglesia, which is Spanish for "church," as he was a priest). He was willing to spend $1,000, so I went and looked for items around $1,000 that I'd want to trade for. I found, of all things, a Boosted Board.

(By this point, I was still sitting at the bus stop. It was 11 p.m.)

Fair enough if you have no idea what a Boosted Board is. It's essentially a battery-powered skateboard. You can use them to travel dangerously fast around the city. I only knew what they were because a high-profile YouTuber had just gotten one and become famous for riding around New York City on his board. (Bad news: Boosted was a venture-backed startup that went out of business in 2020, so no luck buying a new one if you're interested.)

Sitting at that sad bus stop in full view of my broken car, I started furiously typing out messages to lock down the trade. It looked like it was in the bag, so I let Iglesia know.

Then, of course, the board fell through.

I went on a spiral making offers for every board I could find. Not only did I have to find an item for $1,000, but I had to find someone who was willing to make the handoff for the item tonight. I managed to find another one that was listed at $1,200 and I talked him down to $1,100. I let Iglesia know he could go try to pick it up and negotiate further, but he said no. He only had $1,000 to spend.

Could he just give me money? Desperate to make the trade, I put my long explanation into Google Translate and sent it to him. No, I couldn't take money. I needed to trade for another item. I could help find something. I'd try to make it for $1,000. But I wanted a skateboard.

*I need the title to go skateboarding*, he responded to me.

I got the gist.

I sent him the listing again for the skateboard. $1,100 and the address. He agreed.

Then I left my sad vigil and went to eat a very late dinner.

While I was at dinner, I compulsively checked my messages. Iglesia seemed to know what he was doing. I sent photos of the board he needed to pick up. I told the person selling the board a guy was coming for it and that he had cash. I just hoped when the two of them met face-to-face, they wouldn't be too weirded out that I wasn't there.

When photos of the board came through from Iglesia, I was beyond thrilled. We set a time to meet—right after I finished my dinner—and back I went to the car. He was waiting for me, and I handed over the keys and title. He signed the title by flashlight. The van still wouldn't start, but he and his buddy seemed to have a plan. Having spent way too many of the last 48 hours hanging out next to this van, I got out of there.

The next morning, Bobby and I biked past the parking spot where the van had been. It had vanished in the night, presumably with Iglesia.

After I knew the trade had been made and the car had been picked up, I made a video about everything that had happened.

My intent was just to keep my followers updated, but the effect that video had was instantaneous and terrible. People started being extremely negative about the couple who had traded me the van. They were worried I'd been scammed, and they were mad. They even started sending messages to the couple, calling them out.

The Internet is a beautiful and terrible thing.

Once I saw what was happening, I felt horrible. My intent had never been any kind of callout. Not only was I not even remotely mad at them, but it also wasn't their responsibility. Remember: As the person trading, you get a chance to ask questions and do your homework, but once the trade is made, the outcome is on you.

---

## No tradebacks.

---

This was my first experience with Internet mitigation. I had to get on all my channels and tell people to knock it off. I then made a video that spoke really positively about the couple, thanking them for being such excellent supporters of the Project. Eventually, the furor died down, but it was unkind to the couple who had been so invested in the Project. Even now, thinking about it saddens me.

At the same time, this was inarguably a down trade. That hadn't happened to me before. I'd gone from a new and desirable iPhone to a Dodge Caravan that wouldn't start, which taught me a fundamental lesson of trading:

---

## Not all trades work out.

---

If you're going to get into trading, you have to be prepared. Not all trades are going to go your way. While you want to do everything you can to make smart trades, do it long enough and stuff will go wrong. Fortunately, making one bad trade doesn't matter. It's what you do with that bad trade that counts. How are you going to get unblocked? How are you going to move forward?

What I'd done with my mediocre trade was get myself a battery-powered skateboard. Now I had to figure out what that meant for the next step in the Trade Me Project.

# CHAPTER 7

# NO TRADEBACKS

Down trades are the worst.

I'd been on such a high. All the press and excitement around the van arriving in San Francisco (before I discovered it was not operational) had been amazing. There was a picture of me sitting in the driver's seat grinning that made the news everywhere. Things had been going so well and the trades had all been happening so quickly that this first major setback really knocked me off my feet. I even took a day off to recoup.

The thing is, sometimes down trades are necessary. When you get stuck, the most important thing is to get yourself unblocked. Insisting on a trade that got me back to where I was with the iPhone 11 Pro Max on value would have meant that the Trade Me Project was over—or at least significantly delayed. The most important thing to remember is that down trades aren't the end of the story. Sometimes, to work your way up, you first have to go back down. I'd love to say this was the only down trade I made, but that would prove to be wishful thinking.

---

**Sometimes, the only way to unblock yourself is to make a down trade.**

---

After a day off digital marketplaces and social media, I was ready to dive back in.

*The Boosted Board isn't that bad*, I told myself. *There's definitely a market for it.*

The problem was that while it was cool, the board was solidly a Type B item. (See Chapter 3.) Someone would want it—but a very specific someone. I was going to have to look hard to find them.

I wanted out of broken-down vans and specialty rec gear and back into something predictable I knew I could trade. I began looking for brand-name electronics. This was ironic, considering how stuck I'd felt just a few weeks ago when I was trading computers and headphones. But at least this would put me back into something predictable and desirable.

Unlike with the last Type B item (the snowboard), I didn't have the patience to wait for someone to come to me. I began proactively looking for items I knew I wanted. That's how I found a guy on Facebook Marketplace who'd listed something that caught my eye. A day or so later, he DMed me directly and said he'd be interested in the trade, offering me a MacBook Pro—a newer model than last time. Perfect.

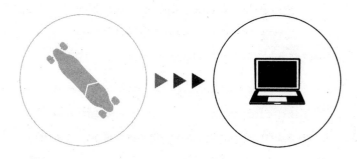

## TRADE 16: BOOSTED BOARD FOR A 2017 MACBOOK PRO

The Trade Me Project was kind of the perfect storm of everything I naturally love to do. It sat right at the nexus of my strategic skills and my ability to negotiate—plus my ability to be obsessively dedicated to making things work.

Here's what I mean by that. When I was in my early twenties, I applied for a job at Apple. I had some of the qualifications for the job—but not all of them, especially the required knowledge of certain software programs. I knew if I disclosed that to the recruiter, they wouldn't let me move on to the next round.

Instead of telling him I didn't know the programs, I emailed a bunch of professors who taught these subjects in the DC area and asked if they could teach me everything they knew in a few hours. One finally agreed, so I went to his office, and he explained an entire course in a few hours.

I got the job and almost doubled my salary.

After having sent hundreds of thousands of messages for the Trade Me Project, I'm confident I can sell literally anything. All I need is the opening, and I'll figure it out.

---

**The most important thing about negotiation is listening to what the other person is telling you.**

---

People like to believe they're savvier than they are, but they'll accidentally reveal all kinds of things about themselves that give you an advantage. Understanding the other person's psychology is the key to making a trade happen.

---

**However, just to be clear, negotiation is never about tricking the other person.**

---

Fundamental to good trading is believing the trade is in the best interest of both parties. I never want to take advantage of someone, but I do want both of us to feel like we've won. People *love* to feel like they've won.

I'm always trying to trade for an item that's at least 10% more valuable than the item I currently have. The Trade Me Project's viewers always think I "win" the trade because I'm getting more monetary value. In reality, it isn't always monetary value that makes an item desirable to someone. Sometimes, it's the item itself. There might be a memory tied to a specific item or someone might need that item right when I'm offering it for trade. Whether it's nostalgia, timing, or ease of acquisition, value works in many ways that aren't just related to money.

To be able to listen to what the other person is telling you, you have to communicate—a lot. This is a balance. On one hand, you don't want to give people too much time to think through a trade. Overthinking = backing out. On the other hand, you want to give people as many opportunities as you can to reveal themselves. In trading, knowledge is power.

By the time I was trying to trade away the Boosted Board, I'd had a little practice communicating with potential trading partners. I was much more efficient than I used to be at figuring out what I needed to know, making the pitch, and closing the deal.

## 1. Ask for the specs of their item.

Before you get in too deep, make sure the item they have is worth trading for. Obviously, what that means totally depends on the item itself, but there are a few commonalities. For example, what's the year, make, and model of the item?

Computers that are only a year or two old will have way more value than the same model from eight years ago. Computers with more memory will also have more value. Knowing exactly what you're dealing with will help you research the market for the item, giving you an idea of dollar value. If you're not sure, do your research or ask an expert. You don't know what you don't know.

## 2. Check the condition of their item—and always get pictures.

Condition really matters, especially for collectible items like shoes. If the item is utilitarian, like a vacuum, it matters less, but you still want items that work and look nice. If there are dings and scuffs, can you fix them? While you should ask the other person to disclose any issues, you should always, *always* ask for pictures and videos. Lots of them.

## 3. Make sure any necessary accessories are actually included.

Charging cords, adapters, battery packs—make sure everything that's supposed to come with the item is there. Again, you might have to do some research to make sure you know all the accessories that should be included. Then there's the stuff that's nice to have but not necessary: cases, boxes, dust bags, etc.

## 4. Get third-party verification.

This one isn't strictly necessary, but there are going to be items that need an outside opinion to green-light the trade. Sneakers are a great example, but this can also apply as you move into high-value items. Jewelry (more on this later) and cars are great examples.

## 5. Ask where the item's located.

Shipping can make life really, really complicated. Sometimes, it's worth it; sometimes, it isn't. You need to know ASAP so you can factor in the cost and hassle.

You can ask for this information in pieces, but it's best to check all this stuff as quickly as possible before you get into the real negotiation. You don't want to waste your time on items that don't meet your criteria. Unless you're lucky, it takes vetting many, many items before you'll find something worth trading for, so you want to be able to go through this part of the process quickly.

That's exactly what I did in this case. The guy interested in the Boosted Board told me early on that he had a 2017 MacBook Pro with a touchbar to trade. He said it came new in the box and was in "super clean condition."

*Hi - what are the specs?* I asked him. *Do you have photos as well?*

He sent over a bunch of photos, including one of the handy Overview that Macs provide in the Settings showing the memory, graphics, etc. The screen was 15 inches. One photo showed the charger and box. Everything was in order, and it did look brand new.

Specs acquired, condition verified, accessories included.

Not wanting to be too demanding, now it was my turn to sell. He asked how much the Boosted Board had cost. I had already done my research (always come prepared to a negotiation). I didn't give one price. I'd already looked up about how much a MacBook Pro with those specs cost, and it was more than my board. Sometimes. New, the board had cost $1,200, which I told him. *However,* the board was sold out everywhere. A huge point in my favor. I led with that little fact. So he couldn't actually buy it for $1,200. In terms of resale, there was a range, which I also told him. Then I provided him with the screenshot of a carefully selected example of the same board, which happened to be listed at $2,299.00. Based on my research, that was pretty close to what the MacBook Pro was valued at originally. I didn't point out the price on that one to him. I let the listing speak for itself.

He told me he could get $1,400 for the laptop (good luck!), and it had cost him $2,450. Noted.

Now to check the final piece of info—where was the laptop? If he was local, that would be amazing, but if he wasn't, it wasn't a big deal. Laptops are easy to ship and insure. Had logistics been more complex, I'd have checked this earlier on.

*Cool where are you located,* I asked him.

He was in Oregon, which meant that shipping was required but not too tricky.

Secretly, I was in. I liked the laptop, and it would be a good trade for me. I'd go up in value, and I'd exchange a Type B item for a solidly Type A item (something others would want).

I went into full sales mode. I sent a bunch of photos and videos of the board. I acted casual about it, but I made sure to send media with good lighting and a cool setup. He even complimented me on the awesome rug I'd put the board on to photograph it.

---

### Great photos and a knowledgeable description go a long way.

---

I talked about how fun it was to have taken the board for a spin (thus proving it worked). He asked the mileage, and I told him I thought it was less than 10 miles, but I'd go check. Then he told me something very interesting:

*I will use that more than I will use my MacBook. I have 2 of them.*

Oh buddy.

The board actually had way less than 10 miles on it—only 4. Which I promptly told him, making the board sound even better. Then I said:

*I just wish the laptop was 2018.*

Just planting the seed.

I followed that with a screenshot of the board's mileage to confirm. I was ready to make the trade.

*I don't mind paying for the shipping. I can send you a label you can slap on the box today.*

When you're ready to make the deal, go for it. Remember to pull the limited levers you have—paying for shipping and your willingness to do the work—to get it done.

## Be Patient

People hate being sold on things. Within society, there's a general concept that people shouldn't be "sold," and the folks pushing for those sales are typically shown in a negative light. The classic example is the used car salesman.

People also want to think that something was their idea. In cases where you're attempting to "close a trade," it's very important to understand where you have room to push and where you need to give the person space to think. If you come on too strong out of the gate, people will sometimes clam up, and you won't be able to reopen the idea. When you find yourself sitting back and waiting, sometimes the only surefire way to get the conversation back is to send a message that makes the other person feel like the ball is still in their court. You can send photos and videos or ask clarifying questions—anything that will drive the conversation forward but also make the other person feel like you're being helpful in their decision-making (while not pushing).

Then he went dark on me. Not for long, but he responded saying he'd been busy.

Not a problem—did he have other questions?

He didn't respond again.

*Hey—just let me know if you aren't interested so I can head on to the next person.*

I was applying a little pressure but also saving myself time from chasing after this guy.

No response.

So, I called him.

---

**Respect people's boundaries, but don't be afraid to reach out.**

---

Instagram and Facebook DMs are pretty easy to ignore. If you want to get a trade done, reach out and try to get the other person to talk live. Then there's no waiting on messages to be read or people to respond. Plus, it also gives the other person more opportunities to talk.

In our 10-minute phone call, I learned a few things about this guy.

He was interested in the skateboard because he was a skater! In fact, he taught kids to skate at the local skate park. He told me all about his own kids and how much he loved getting the next generation into skateboarding. He told me about growing up skateboarding and what it meant to him. I thought it was really cool, and I was excited to be getting him the board. It would go to a good home, and it seemed like he would love having it.

Then he tried to haggle with me. The computer was valued at *way* more than the board he said, so maybe I could sweeten the deal with cash or throw in something extra? I explained that wasn't how the Trade Me Project worked—trades only. He was really trying to drive a hard bargain, which surprised me given our conversation in the DMs. He'd seemed so sold. I was glad I called because I now realized he wasn't. Or he was sold on the skateboard, but he just wanted to feel better about the deal and see what else he could get.

As he was once again talking through the price disparity between the two items, he let something slip. *He hadn't bought the computer from a retailer.* Actually, he had bought it off a friend for half the sticker price. All his arguments about the money he was losing and why it was a bad deal for him were null and void. It was a pretty equitable deal for him—and he got something he actually wanted out of the exchange rather than having an extra (remember?) computer sitting around gathering dust.

The more insight you have into someone's circumstances, the better you can evaluate how much value each item has for them. The people who really play hardball are also the ones who tend to show their cards. People who don't want to trade or have hard boundaries on price or condition aren't going to compromise and won't waste their time haggling.

## Listen

Being an active listener is a super important aspect of trading that might not seem obvious at first. Oftentimes, people who are on the other end of the trade will let you in on small details about their life (likely without even knowing it) that will help you close the deal in the future. Sometimes, these details are about their living situation, their family, an item they hope to have in the future, the value of the item they currently have, or how they came to own the item in the first place. In learning a bit about the person, you can use this knowledge to understand what might drive them to finally make the trade. *The key to trading is figuring out what people want and what's important to them.* The item's condition?

> Seamless shipping? Exposure on the Trade Me Project's platforms? (Or the opposite: being kept completely off social channels?) Without the answers to those questions, it's very hard to drive a deal across the finish line.

Before you're certain the deal is on, the trick is to keep the other person engaged. The back and forth is meant to help you gauge whether they're committing or leaving. Why are they asking for a better deal? Are they being honest that they actually want the item?

When they slip up, that's when you go for it. I now knew this trade was more valuable to him than the MacBook. I *knew* he was going to do it.

He said he was in and couldn't believe he was doing something so crazy.

I had to go to the post office *now*—before he backed out. Remember: Sometimes, you have to be the person who jumps.

It was the middle of the day and I had meetings. But I knew time was of the essence to close this trade. To save time, I tried to schedule a pickup with UPS instead of waiting until after work to ship it. With every minute that passed, I could tell I was losing my trade partner. Luckily, Bobby—ever the Project's #1 supporter—ordered a Lyft and took the board off to be shipped.

I wish I could say this was the end of the trade, that the guy also drove right to the post office and mailed me the computer with the label I'd sent him. But he didn't. In fact, he went dark on me for three full days. I was sure I'd lost the board.

Trying to get his attention, I sent a bunch of messages and called. *Finally*, he replied—just busy and living the dad life. Fair enough. He was going to get the board in the mail.

Again, I wish this had happened right away, but it was a few more days before the box with the computer got in the mail. In the meantime, the board had arrived at his place. It was so cute—he sent a photo of him beaming, holding the box with the board over his head. He also sent a few videos. Bobby and I loved seeing it.

The computer also arrived—and all's well that ends well.

The lesson I learned here is there are people—many people—who'll really push to sweeten the deal. They want not just a good trade but the *best* trade. They're going to try to get an even better deal, even if you offer them a fair and great one right off the bat. Most often, they'll ask you to throw in money. All you can do is say "No" and pull the levers you have: shipping, logistics, and psychology.

*Just trade for a MacBook Pro already!!!* said one of the comments under a previous video. Bobby grabbed the comment, and we "responded" to it via a new TikTok video.

"Okay!" I said and then cut to my trading partner packaging up his computer, it getting scanned in the mail, and my unboxing it. I explained that this MacBook was much newer than the one from a few trades ago. *Shoot me a follow*, I told my viewers, *and let's get this house!*

In the weeks it had taken to make the last few trades, I'd posted a few videos of filler content. People were used to hearing from me once a week, so I wanted to make sure I kept in touch. I did a short video of my upgrading the setup in my apartment's entryway; I added a new console and then hung some pegs and a mirror. My channel was never going to be DIY-themed, but it was the middle of the pandemic, and no one had anything to do but sit at home and order stuff off Amazon to make their living spaces more bearable.

Then I had a great idea: Why not reach out to Abbie, the girl who I'd originally traded the bobby pin for the earrings and record a conversation? One of the most common questions I got on TikTok was who in their right mind had done the original trade. Who wanted a *bobby pin*? Everyone assumed it had to be fake or someone I knew.

Little did they know.

To clear things up, Abbie and I got on Zoom and had a chat. We talked about how we'd found each other on Facebook but had never met or even spoken to each other outside of Facebook messages. She said she just liked the idea, and the earrings weren't something she'd ever worn or needed. Then I asked her the second most common question I got: Did she still have the bobby pin?

Yes, as it turned out. It was still stuck on the card I'd written thanking her for participating. Her husband, doing some cleanup, had asked if he could put it in the bathroom. Nope! She told him. Not that one.

Then I had the *best* idea. There were so, so many people in my comments saying how much they'd give to have the current trade laptop. I was feeling very emotional reading comments from kids in college who desperately wanted it or professionals who thought it could give them a huge boost. I'd traded for something that many people couldn't afford. The only way they could get a computer this nice might be to do something like strategically trade for it. So I decided I'd do a giveaway.

Of course, I wasn't giving away the laptop I'd just traded for, but I had an extra MacBook from my previous job. I explained the rules of the giveaway: You just had to be following me on Instagram or TikTok and make a video using the hashtag #letsgetthishouse explaining why you should get the laptop.

People were so confused. Was I trading a laptop? Why was I giving it away? Was it the same laptop? Why would I do that? Was I not trading anymore?

My intentions were so good, but I hadn't thought about the giveaway enough. My impulsiveness had created a confusing experience for my followers. Nevertheless, a few hundred people submitted videos. I watched them, chose a couple with a sweet story, cleared my laptop, and sent it. The experience was a great lesson in being thoughtful about how I engaged with my followers, particularly when it came to giving stuff away. Having made a few good videos and run one mediocre giveaway, I decided I had better get back to what I was best at: trading.

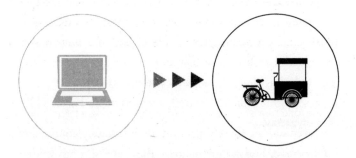

## TRADE 17: 2017 MACBOOK PRO FOR A FERLA ELECTRIC BIKE FOOD CART

Having gone for something safe with the MacBook Pro, my next trade was for the most aggressively Type B item yet.

I'd been poking around Facebook Marketplace when I saw a posting for a food cart that was built around an electric bike. Bobby and I love biking (we don't even own a car), and something about it just spoke to me. It was made by a company called Ferla. Truly, I'd never seen anything like it. It was an electric bike with a enclosed cart on the front. The guy posting it had it for sale in San Francisco, so it seemed perfect.

I reached out to the guy and started my negotiation. A computer for an entire electric food cart might be a tough sell, but I figured he'd have a tough time offloading it. Pretty quickly into our conversation, I realized the guy was listing the bike and cart on behalf of Ferla, the company that made them, because he *worked* there. The ad wasn't a real ad—it was marketing. The bike was listed for sale, but really, they were trying to direct you to their website.

Because this was a company trying to market a product, I had a new lever I could pull. Yes, the teenagers who traded me the final pair of sneakers had been interested in the power of my social media platform because it might give them some exposure. It was a nice bonus.

But for a new startup trying to get their product out there, my reach was a huge selling point. I immediately got the guy on the phone and started selling him.

"I'm just a sales rep," he told me. "But I can intro you to the CEO."

Finding the decision-maker is always key. I had two or three calls with the CEO of Ferla, explaining to him the value of getting Ferla on the Trade Me Project platform. They didn't need the computer, but it wouldn't be wasted. They could use the computer, but they could *really* use millions of people seeing how cool their electric food cart was.

This wasn't a cynical play on my part. I loved the cart, and I believed my platform would be valuable exposure. How valuable? That was hard to measure. The CEO wanted hard metrics proving what Trade Me Project marketing would do for him. I couldn't make any promises related to views, much less sales. All I could do was point him to my content and demos and tell him to read my comments and see how invested and interested people were.

There were moments I was sure I'd lost the trade. He kept asking for more metrics and guarantees. I'd hang up from our calls shaking my head. He wasn't interested enough.

But then another call would always get scheduled. Finally, I found myself on a call negotiating with the *entire team*. It was hilarious and also so amazing to be explaining the ins and outs of the Trade Me Project and how the exposure could amplify their brand. I showed a breakdown of the demographics of my viewers and their engagement. I was on fire—I loved getting to talk about the Project. I had and have such a deep passion for trading and have always been so grateful for people's interest. Getting to make a business case around that was the icing on the cake.

When I got off the phone, I knew I'd crushed it.

Bobby was filming me. I turned around and immediately went "THAT'S HOW IT'S DONE," like I was Jerry Maguire or something. In that moment, I loved everything about the Trade Me Project.

The team signed off, and the trade was made. It felt like the Trade Me Project had reached new heights.

To retrieve the electric food cart, Bobby and I rented a truck and drove down to Los Angeles, where it was located. I teased the trade on a video, showing the door to a warehouse slowly rolling up before going to black. *The biggest trade yet*, I told my followers.

Then I filmed a video with Ferla to document the trade. We took footage of my riding the bike around the warehouse complex, and they gave us a tour of their space with the different models of electric food carts they had available. We got to see the factory and how they made the bikes. It was the first time a true experience was associated with the Trade Me Project. Because of the pandemic, so much of the trading and interaction had been digital, punctuated by brief 30-second meetups. It was amazing to get to spend real time with the people I was trading with while also learning about their business. It all felt so much more real.

People's reactions to the trade were mixed. Some people felt like this was just branded content that would never have happened without my platform. They were partially right, but it wasn't an ad. I wasn't paid money, and we truly did trade. I'd used my platform as a lever to pull, not as something I sold. It helped that the electric food cart had a listed value of $4,000. That helped people see I was going up in value, making better and better trades. Plus, the bike was just cool.

With my new trade in hand, I had a crazy idea I could make my next trade simply by standing with the new cart on the Venice Boardwalk. But as I stood there next to the food cart, dodging buffed-out guys on Rollerblades, I realized I'd miscalculated. People weren't coming to the boardwalk with stuff to trade, especially stuff worth $4,000.

No problem. Bobby and I packed up the electric food cart and drove it six hours back from LA to San Francisco. I started riding the food cart around San Francisco, especially to extremely busy areas. I got signs printed with *Want to trade?* and the Trade Me Project social handles on them that I affixed to the cart.

I'd picked this item because it was expensive, flashy, and weird. It was an item that nearly nobody would want—but someone would. The challenge made me love it even more. To find that one person, I needed as many people as possible to see it. This wasn't an item I could proactively offer to people on Facebook Marketplace—it was a Type B item.

One day, I was riding the electric food cart bike around the city. I'd been doing this more and more often to up my chances. A random guy approached me—could he be the one?—and flagged me down.

"Hey! Demi!" he said.

"Hi," I said back, having no idea who he was.

"We love your videos!" he told me.

"Oh, awesome!" I said, expecting him to tell me about how he'd been watching since the bobby pin days.

"Yeah, my whole team at TikTok is super into them."

His team at *TikTok?* Wait a minute—I got off the bike and started chatting with him. He worked on some team at TikTok, and it turns out the Trade Me Project was popular at the company. Which was surprising because I'd tried to reach out a few times and … never heard back.

That was the first and last time I ever talked to someone at TikTok. People sometimes accuse me of having some kind of inside relationship with the company that helped promote what I was doing, but that couldn't have been further from the truth. My single interaction with anyone who worked there was a random guy on the street who came up as a fan. That was it.

Without the powers that be at TikTok to make my electric food cart trade happen, it looked like it was all up to me. I got back on the bike seat and went peddling off to go find my next trade—and get that house.

## CHAPTER 8

# THE $20,000 NECKLACE THAT SOLD FOR $2,000

I was convinced that trading away the electric food cart would take forever. It would be my weirdest trade ever. It would take weeks—maybe even months!

While I continued to look for the perfect trade, I decided to put together my first FAQ video.

Here's what I said:

*I'm trading a single bobby pin all the way until I get a house. Right now, I'm at a $4,000 electric bike food cart. I get tons of questions about how I actually do this, so I wanted to answer them.*

*The #1 question I get is about how I find people to actually trade with. So this is nothing fancy. It's just Facebook Marketplace. I'll pick San Francisco as my city and then I go to a price range and I'll pick a little bit higher than the item that I had. After that, I pick a category—maybe it's cameras or a bike—and then I start reaching out to people.*

*So, I reach out to thousands of people on Facebook Marketplace who are selling, and then once they reply back, I'll see if they're interested in trading. (Only 1 in 1,000 actually wants to trade.)*

*Some other tips for trading is that typically, people don't like trading in the same category. So if I have a MacBook, no one is going to trade me for a better MacBook because that trade just doesn't make sense for them.*

*Second, people like to stay within name brands. So if they recognize the name brand of the item, they'll typically trade for it. If it's something really obscure they've never heard of, it's usually a harder trade.*

*Third, make sure you do your research. Get videos, photos. Make sure it's real. Make sure no pieces are missing and it's exactly what you expect.*

*If you have any questions I haven't answered, feel free to put them in the comments and I'll try to answer all of them.*

After that video, I had a several of people reach out to tell me they'd started their own trading journey. I still firmly believe that anyone is capable of trading—you just have to be willing to commit.

I then closed the video by teasing that my new trade was coming this week because after all that worry, I'd managed to find my next trade that very same day.

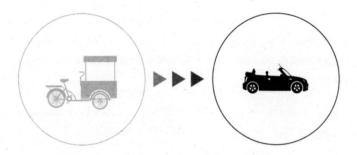

## TRADE 18: FERLA ELECTRIC BIKE FOOD CART FOR A 2006 MINI COOPER CONVERTIBLE

Sometimes, the stars align and trading is unexpectedly incredibly simple. Not often, but it happens.

Trading that electric bike food cart couldn't have been more straightforward. My publicity ploy worked, and the interest was inbound (as it often is for Type B items). One day, out of the blue, I got an Instagram DM from a guy named Lucas.

*I'll trade you my 2006 Mini Cooper S convertible*, it said.

A Mini Cooper? This could be big.

However, having had experience trading cars, I knew not to get too excited too quickly.

*Hey Lucas. Where are you located and how many miles does it have on it? Any issues?*

Bad news off the bat: He was in Wilmington, North Carolina—only 2,900 miles from San Francisco. However, the car had 145,000 miles on it and no issues except that some of the clear coat was bubbling, which was only a cosmetic issue. If it all checked out, this could be an incredible trade.

I asked for photos, which Lucas sent, and immediately set to work trying to figure out logistics. The Mini Cooper looked amazing for being more than 10 years old. It was a classic hunter green with black leather bucket seats and a black convertible cloth top.

I asked Lucas if he had the title, and he did. We arranged to FaceTime later that night to discuss details.

I wasn't sure what to expect considering this was coming together so quickly, but Lucas was so nice. The only thing I couldn't figure out was why he wanted to trade his zippy, well-maintained Mini Cooper for my food cart. I loved the food cart, but the value didn't exactly seem equal. Then he told me he wanted to start an ice cream business on the beach during the pandemic. The food cart was perfect for his new venture. Mystery solved.

Trades can be so hard, but sometimes, they just fall in your lap. When the interest is inbound and the other person's questions are minimal, it's the best.

By now, after having talked to thousands of people, I can tell within just a few messages where someone is on the Scale of Interest.

You don't often get people who are already sold, but when you do, go for it. These "already sold" trades come from all types of people—trading doesn't skew rich or poor or young or old. Trading is a great option for those low on physical cash (the standard currency most use to trade) and for those with an excess of physical items to trade. I find that it's important to not judge the person but to instead look for context clues they give you from their conversations.

---

**Never judge a fellow trader—
good trades come in all forms.**

---

Based on our conversation, I could tell Lucas no longer wanted the Mini Cooper, and selling used cars is a hassle (something I'll discuss more in future trades). The electric bike food cart would be useful to him, and this was an easy way of getting one. He didn't necessarily need to go find the best food cart out there; this was a convenient way of solving his present need.

I was totally in. The Mini Cooper would be really fun to trade—but what was I going to do about the fact it was in North Carolina?

This is where I unlocked a new strategy: You don't always need to physically have the items sent to you. Instead of shipping the car across the country all the way to California, why not just leave it in North Carolina and trade it from there? I just needed to find a safe place to store it on the East Coast before it could go to its new home. Why had I never thought of this before?

---

## To save on shipping, trade in place.

---

But the electric bike food cart did need to get to Lucas in North Carolina. I went to Home Depot and bought a bunch of plywood. I was going to build a crate to ship the bike in. After having solved so many problems in the course of the trades, I think I felt that if anyone could do it, it was me.

So, I got all the wood together in my backyard and started sketching the dimensions of the crate. I'm sure my neighbors wondered what we were doing.

What *were* we doing?

Getting way out of our league is what we were doing. I have a lot of skills but not the skills necessary to build a crate that is sturdy enough to ship a six-foot-tall electric bike food cart across the country. The lesson is that some things are better left to the pros. We loaded up all the unused plywood on our bikes and took it back to Home Depot. Then I got on uShip.

uShip, which you've probably never heard of, has been one of my biggest assets during the trading journey. It's essentially a platform where you can post your shipping needs and then various vendors will bid on the job. The marketplace is an incredible way to get fast, reliable, and safe shipping anywhere in the United States. After many trades with complicated shipping, I can proudly say I'm uShip's #1 fan.

But there was one more complication with the Mini. What was I going to do about the title? I did some research and found there's a cost every time you sign over the title on a car. Rather than doing the paperwork over and over again (and also because I couldn't spend any money), I came up with a strategy to save time and money on title exchanges.

Each time I traded a car going forward, I'd have the original owner sign the transfer and leave the new owner's name blank. This way, my name would never be on it, I'd never have to go to the DMV, and the new owner could simply sign the same paper to transfer the vehicle directly to themselves.

Unfortunately, I hadn't come up with this strategy for the minivan trade. After I received several toll road bills from the priest who had ended up with the minivan, I learned I needed to be very meticulous in making sure the title was actually signed and I wasn't liable for any bills or issues. (I reached out to him over and over to let him know about the toll charges, and he did end up paying them.)

To make sure I wasn't paying bridge tolls on two coasts, I had Lucas give me the title with the new owner's name blank.

Once the cart arrived at Lucas's house, a friend of mine from high school, Christina, went to get the Mini. Once the trade was safely at her house, I made a video to announce the new trade. People were *so* excited about it. The food cart had been kind of a tough sell to my audience, but my followers got the Mini right away. It was so cute and looked great for its age.

The comments on my video announcement were amazing:

**Sarah:** *The fact that a convertible Mini Cooper is my dream car and you got it through trades is amazing!! I'm kinda jealous* 😔😂

**Adrian:** *BRO, a tiny metal object to a whole car!* 😄👍

**Matt:** *That's a good freaking trade!*

**Rochelle:** *The fact that you've gone from 1 single bobby pin to $6500 is crazy* 😵 *I can't wait to see the house x*

Neither could I.

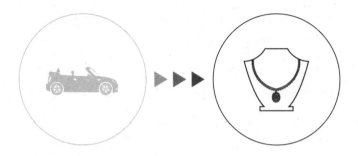

## TRADE 19: 2006 MINI COOPER CONVERTIBLE FOR A DIAMOND AND SAPPHIRE NECKLACE

Yet again, I could leverage the power of a brand name. The Mini Cooper had plenty of inbound interest, and I felt like I was in a good position to make a strong trade. Also, unlike with the van, there wasn't pressure to move the Mini Cooper quickly. It was safe with my friend, so I had time to look for the best trade.

Just like with the last trade, this one came to me. After posting an Instagram Reel of the Mini driving off into the sunset, I got a DM from a woman named Corbin. She'd messaged me a few months earlier back in June asking about trade strategy, but with so many messages, I'd missed hers completely. Corbin was just generally interested in the Trade Me Project and how it all worked (which I loved!).

The first message Corbin sent me about the Mini Cooper read like this: *I would love to trade you for this. I have a 6ct diamond and sapphire "tennis" necklace I would be willing to trade.*

Then she included a picture of the necklace, which was in a beautiful case and looked almost exactly like the one Rose threw in the ocean at the end of *Titanic*.

She followed the photo up with a few more messages: *I live in Virginia, so I could easily pick up the car in North Carolina. Please let me know if you are interested! I love following your journey!!*

I asked her about the estimated value and if she had any documentation. She'd had the necklace appraised at 13 carats of stone for $28,000 (*twenty-eight grand!*) by one jeweler. Then she had another jeweler grade it. That jeweler said there were only 6 carats of diamonds, rather than 13 carats, as she had originally told me. Even at 6 carats, she was positive it was worth more than $7,000.

She also sent photos of the appraisal but said there was no GIA. I googled it. GIA meant a Gemological Institute of America Diamond Grading Report. These are in-depth reports about the quality of the stones you pay to get that are legit. If you want to buy or sell fine diamonds, they're really helpful to have.

*Ah any reason there is no GIA? Where did you get it from?*

Corbin told me she got it from an estate sale. It hadn't come with a GIA report, and she had only ever gotten it appraised by local jewelers.

I was so fascinated by the necklace. It was beautiful, but I didn't know anything about jewelry. I was also worried about fraud—like shoes, jewelry can be faked. I hadn't had to worry about that for a while. You don't have to worry about fake cars or fake cameras, but a diamond and sapphire necklace? Verifying the authenticity of shoes was one thing, but making sure a diamond necklace was real—one potentially worth almost $30,000—was a whole other deal.

After doing some research and discussing it with Bobby, I asked Corbin if she could get another appraisal. I'd actually gone to the University of Virginia in Charlottesville, very close to where Corbin lived, so I was familiar with the area. We discussed a few different jewelers she could take it to.

I also sent her photos and videos of the Mini. All she requested was the VIN so she could pull the Carfax report and make sure it hadn't been in any accidents, etc. I made sure to disclose it was manual, which wasn't a problem for her. She asked if I had driven it, which was a hard no because 1) I can't drive stick, and 2) I'd never even seen it in person. However, my friend assured me it was a great car.

*My husband is 6'4" and says he hopes we can trade with you so he can have his "hair blow in the wind,"* she wrote back. *I'm not sure how he will pick up our 2-year-old from daycare but ok …*

I laughed so hard. It was so fun trading with someone who was genuinely excited and curious about the Project and trading. Corbin had even been paying attention to the comments on my previous videos and noted that most people thought I'd only be able to trade the Mini for another car or maybe a boat.

Because she was so interested in the behind-the-scenes mechanics, I even showed her some of the other trade options I had for the Mini, which included a tow trailer and, of all things, an industrial-sized ice cream maker. Tempting—but maybe even more Type B than the electric bike food cart. Meanwhile, she worked on getting another appraisal. I even coached her on getting footage that could be included in the eventual video we made.

The new appraisal came back strong. The gold alone was $3,600 and the sapphire centerpiece was $4,500. It would appraise "well over" $5,000, and he provided a warranty for the appraisal. When the final documentation came through, the jeweler had appraised it at $19,500.

I was ecstatic. The leap in value was huge. Now I just had to get Corbin the Mini Cooper.

It was about a six-hour drive from Wilmington to Richmond. Corbin could drive about two hours to Rocky Mount but not farther. I was willing to do anything—short of flying there in the middle of a pandemic and driving it myself. Instead, I decided to leverage the power of the Trade Me Project network.

I put out a call on social media: I had a trade, and I needed help transporting the Mini. I hinted the next trade was amazing—we just had to get the car to its new location Immediately, people started offering to help. It was *incredible*. I'd already experienced the positive power of the Internet during my sneaker era, but this was a whole new level.

First, I heard from Madison. She was another fan of the Trade Me Project who lived in nearby Charlotte. She offered to drive to Wilmington to meet my friend Christina and pick up the Mini Cooper as well as the title and then drive the car to Rocky Mount, halfway between Wilmington and Richmond, where Corbin would be waiting for her.

While the Internet can be a terrible place (fun stories to come), it also can be amazing. Even without the Internet, trading requires a high degree of trust. The number of times that trust has paid off so far outweighs the one and only time I've ever been scammed. Throughout the course of the Project, I've been shown time and time again how truly generous people can be.

---

**While you always have to do your homework, a necessary part of trading is trust.**

---

To make sure we were all on the same page, I initiated a FaceTime call with Madison, Christina, Corbin, and me. All four of us got on together, exchanged contact information, mapped out the route, and decided on meeting points. The planning felt like we were on a secret spy mission.

The next day, Madison set off from Charlotte and was dropped off in Wilmington, where she picked up the Mini Cooper and the title. Then she drove up to Rocky Mount, where Corbin and her husband were waiting. Madison handed over the keys and made sure Corbin signed the title. The trade was complete.

When the necklace came in the mail, I couldn't believe it. I unboxed it on camera. It just didn't seem real. I opened up the red box and the appraisal. There it was. One giant sapphire and 127 individual diamonds for a total of 7.83 carats appraised at $19,500. As I said on the video—*insane.*

The video got tons of views. It was such a flashy item and so unexpected. People were hyped, leaving comments and chatting back and forth:

> **Isabelle:** *at first I was like: "how did u go from a car back to a box" Me after her opening the box:* 👁 👄 👁

> **Kainoa:** *Ummmm you had 19k necklace traded through the mail?! AFTER YOU ALMOST LOST THE SHOES IN THE MAIL?!?!*

(An excellent point.)

> **Naty:** *Let me go get a Bobby pin real quick*

And then the winner:

> **Victoria:** *But I thought the old lady dropped it in the ocean in the end?*

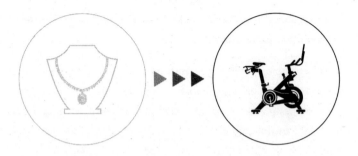

## TRADE 20: DIAMOND & SAPPHIRE NECKLACE FOR A PELOTON V3

I wasn't sure how trading the diamond necklace would go. Would it be easy because of all the attention it had gotten as well as its undeniable value? It would be easy for someone to turn around and just sell it. Or would it be hard because of concerns around authenticity?

Then I experienced the first true, serious public failure of the Trade Me Project.

Yes, the van hadn't gone exactly as planned, but the decrease in value for the next trade was negligible. I'd been able to contain the impact and quickly trade back up. This time, I was screwed.

As I started looking for trades, it became clear that offering to trade jewelry on Facebook Marketplace set off alarm bells for almost everyone. The second I mentioned a trade for a diamond necklace, people were no longer interested. After all, jewelry is one of the most faked items for resale.

Realizing how difficult the trade was going to be, I quickly decided I was willing to make a down trade to unblock myself and arranged to meet up with a man who had offered to trade a white painter van for the necklace.

We agreed to meet at a jeweler in Oakland so he could get an independent appraisal and verify the value before handing off the keys to the van.

That isn't what happened.

I stood at the jewelry counter with my new potential trader as we patiently waited for the jeweler to look at each stone through a magnifying glass. After what felt like hours (it was probably only 15 minutes), the jeweler let us know that the necklace was not worth $19,500—but instead only $2,500.

This is how I learned that the appraised value and the actual retail value of a piece of jewelry—what you can sell it for on the open market—are totally different dollar amounts. Fortunately, the guy I was supposed to trade with could tell I had no idea. I wasn't trying to pull a fast one on him at all; if anything, I was more shocked and sad than he was.

In that moment, I knew I'd never be able to trade this necklace for anything close to $19,500.

## Educate Yourself

Whenever you can, become a "subject matter expert" in your item and learn everything you can about the item you have. Knowing about your item will help you understand the true value of what you have to ensure you make a great trade for yourself, and your expertise will allow you to be perceived as knowledgeable to the person you're attempting to trade with. In many cases, any sign of wavering might make people back out, so being able to answer their questions is important. Finally, you also want to be an expert in the items you're trading *for*. Knowing what you can get will help prevent you from making a bad trade.

Once the true value of the necklace was revealed, I think I exchanged two or three more words with the potential van trader. It was clear the trade was off.

From there, I did what I'd always done: put my head down and got back to work. My job now was to get as many different appraisals as possible for the necklace—to see if I could get anything higher than a $2,500 value for it.

Obviously, I couldn't sell it, but I had to act like I was interested in selling it so jewelers would give me a pricing estimate. I spent hours at a few of them, going back and forth. It was time wasted. They all said the exact same thing: $2,500.

What was I going to do?

My bad options weren't even options. Some of the jewelers wanted to buy it to cut it up into pieces and sell the materials. Fine, except I couldn't sell it. The RealReal offered $5,000 for it, but consignment seemed really dangerous. What if it didn't sell? But I couldn't sell it anyway. I had to trade, and I absolutely couldn't lie and misrepresent the necklace at its insurance-appraised value. Anyone who took it needed to know its market value too.

Gone were my dreams of midrange cars or speed boats. I'd down-traded once before, but this one hurt. I was sending myself back into the low thousands, where I'd been five trades and two months ago.

## Be Open to Restrategizing

Every trade requires a strategy. Sometimes, you might've mapped out a strategy for a particular trade and you still continue to hit a wall. The reasons you might not be making a trade can vary greatly. Other times, you might have overvalued the item you're trying to trade (i.e., you have a 1999 Ford Escape worth $2,000, but you're only looking to trade for items worth $5,000). Instead of sending out hundreds more messages, take a moment to restrategize. This can include picking a different item to trade for, changing the location of your trades, or changing the platform you're using. Any of these actions might help you unlock your next trade. Many times, knocking on the same door over and over won't actually give you a different answer. But if you switch the door you're knocking on, someone might answer.

After a lot of searching, I finally found someone on Facebook Marketplace who was interested in the necklace. Sam and I arranged to meet down the street from my house, where he explained he was moving from San Francisco to New York and needed to offload his Peloton ASAP.

It was clear he absolutely didn't want my necklace (I didn't either), but he did want the cash.

So, we got in separate Lyfts and drove over to that same jewelry store in Oakland so he could verify the price and authenticity of the piece.

Once Sam had verified the necklace was worth $2,500, Bobby and I rented a car and drove over to Sam's apartment. The Peloton would only fit in the back of the car with the trunk open, so I sat in the trunk with the Peloton to make sure it didn't fall out. It was chaos driving through the city. Every time we hit a bump the Peloton's screen would smash into the window. I gave the Peloton a spin when we got home. While it was fun, it wasn't a $20,000 diamond necklace.

When I finally had to post the video of my new trade, people were shocked.

**Louise:** *Girl you went from a whole car to a stationary bike* 😭😭💀

This was a real low point. I'd gone through so many hoops to get the necklace and wasted so much time. Everyone hated the Peloton, but I was relieved. It was a bad consolation prize, but at least I was on solid ground again.

## Trading Items to Avoid

1. **Collectibles:** Anything collectible is (by the nature of it being a collectible) of more value to a very specific set of people who collect it and, therefore, not valuable to the "run of the mill" person who doesn't have that collection. Examples include playing cards, baseball cards, coins, stamps, vinyl, wine, dolls, and books.

2. **Antiques:** Every antique has a widely varying, risky value associated with it. While some antiques have a high dollar value, the ability to do the following is going to be difficult:

   - Find that item

   - Understand its value

   - Find another person who understands the true value

3. **Jewelry:** The second it's purchased, the resale value of jewelry goes down significantly. While the insurance price (the price someone is willing to insure it for if it is lost or stolen) might still be high, this isn't the value you'll be able to get if you sell it. (This one I learned the hard way.)

4. **Vehicles with "salvage" titles or more than 200,000 miles:** While I've traded many, many vehicles in the last few years, those with more than 200,000 miles on them or vehicles with "salvage" titles risk significant mechanical issues and are (in my opinion) never worth the risk associated with them.

5. **Similar items:** What do I mean by this? While this might not seem apparent at first, items that are too similar don't make for good trades. For example, if I were to have a MacBook from 2013 to trade, I'd never be able to trade it for another MacBook or even anything remotely close to a MacBook. This is because it's too obvious to both traders who's going to get the better end of the deal; in most cases, a MacBook from 2015 is going to be better than a MacBook from 2013.

6. **Items that don't hold value:** While people talk a lot about the value of an item when you buy it, they don't often talk about the value of an item when you trade it (or resell it). When you think about items that lose their value, most people think about cars: "The second you drive a new car off the lot, they lose value." It's worth noting that people who are trading are only interested in the value of the item as it stands today.

# CHAPTER 9

# SIR, MAY I PLEASE HAVE A TINY CABIN?

After the highs and lows of my diamond necklace, I had no idea what to expect with my next trade. I was glad the Peloton had an established market around it. This time, there was no question as to my item's monetary value. Too bad that number was way, way lower than where I wanted it to be, but down trading is just part of the game.

Good thing that at this point, I was used to starting over.

> **To keep trading, you have to be willing to restrategize, including making down trades.**

Once I refocused, I went back to all my socials and posted Stories saying I was still looking for another trade. A woman named Kasey reached out to me on Instagram and said she had a Mustang she was maybe willing to trade.

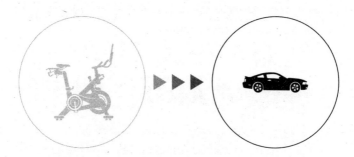

## TRADE 21: PELOTON V3 FOR A 2006 FORD MUSTANG GT DELUXE

I asked Kasey where she was located (Mount Vernon, Washington) and if she could send me pictures. My luck trading cars so far had been 50-50. If it all checked out, I was willing to roll the dice again.

The next day, Kasey sent me photos and more details:

*It was a stormy Washington night so I didn't get pictures yesterday but will do it after work. I will fully disclose that it does have 200K miles, but even rating it as low as possible on Kelly Blue Book it was between $3000 and $4000 for a private sale. Still runs and my husband upgraded to a truck so we just don't need it.*

The photos were awesome. The Mustang was metallic silver with two black racing stripes over the hood and roof. It looked really cool. Kasey let me know it needed a new battery, which should come in a few days. While it seemed like I was getting the better end of the deal, her reasoning made sense to me. I asked Kasey for her address and then posted the job on uShip to start getting shipping quotes for the Peloton.

## The Scale of Interest

Within the first three messages a person sends, you'll be able to understand how likely they are to make a trade. On the far left of this scale (the least likely) is the person who already has "NO TRADES" written on their listing. This means that under no circumstance will this person ever accept a trade. Slightly right of that is the person that says "No" to a trade but then asks for more clarifying information. For example: "Not interested in a trade, but how many miles are on the car?" These people can sometimes be convinced. This is followed by the farthest right on the scale (the most likely): the people who'll reach out to you to trade directly. Inbound interest is a rare gift and should be valued. These are definitely the easier trades to make—and the most fun!

There are so many people who've helped out the Trade Me Project, but this is a special shout-out to all my friends who stored weird things at their houses, especially cars. This time, another friend of mine, Laura, who lives in nearby Seattle, offered to keep the Mustang at her house while I figured out the next trade. She'd drive to Kasey's and pick up the Mustang while I'd ship the Peloton to Kasey. All Kasey had to do was hand over the keys and sign the title, and the trade would be totally taken care of.

---

## Handling logistics and shipping is a major lever to pull for trades.

---

Making things as easy as possible for Kasey helped facilitate the trade. She even asked what kind of paperwork we needed to do, and at this point, I was experienced at transferring car titles. She was excited to send the Mustang off to a new home, and I was excited to be back in automobiles. The Mustang would stay in Seattle while I looked for my next trade.

**Don't move big items unless you have to.
(You don't want to arrange for shipping twice.)**

It had taken me about three weeks to update my social media accounts between the Peloton and the Mustang, so my followers had gotten antsy. I received many comments from people who were worried I'd ghosted them after the necklace debacle. Not the case. I was just being extra, extra careful to make sure everything was in place before I made any announcements. No more "I've made a huge mistake" videos.

From here on out, I wouldn't be making trades every other day or once a week. High-value trades take time, and I wasn't willing to risk the Project on another wild card again.

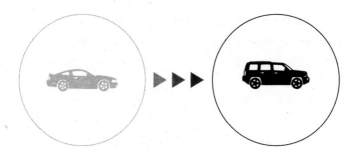

## TRADE 22: 2006 FORD MUSTANG GT DELUXE FOR A 2011 JEEP PATRIOT SPORT

The power of a brand name will never stop surprising me. With a brand name comes a community based solely around that brand—and each time, finding that community pays off.

I knew, of course, that people loved Mustangs, but I thought the antique models were the only ones that really held their value. This was a 2006, so I figured it wasn't old or new enough to generate a lot of interest. As it turned out, that wasn't true. People love a Mustang, even a gently used one from 10 years ago.

My followers were *so* excited about the Mustang. I got so many comments on my videos and tons of inbound interest. People were truly enamored. If the car had been a Honda Civic, even a newer model with fewer miles, I don't think people would have been as excited. As it turns out, Mustangs are just really popular.

Unfortunately, the most active target demographic for a Mustang does seem to be 16-year-old boys. I know because I got a ton of messages from them on Instagram that said things like, *I want to drive a Mustang! I'll give you anything!* I loved the enthusiasm, but their lack of items of equal value meant that any trade was a nonstarter. Sifting through those DMs ate up a ton of my time.

---

**Always keep your core demographic in mind when you're looking at an item.**

---

As I read through all the messages, it was clear a Mustang was the "dream car" for many people.

While it wasn't an item they'd be able to spend $5,000 on, the idea of trading for a Mustang using something they already had in their garage was enticing. There were also features of this specific car that made it even more desirable to people (mostly, I'm guessing, the flashy racing stripes).

Another element of the market around cars specifically is that selling and buying them is a pain. New cars require making so many choices, doing a lot of haggling, and filling out tons of paperwork. It's confusing, unpleasant, and time-consuming. Buying used cars is about the same, except with a slightly better price point. Hence all the apps and websites trying to make buying and selling cars more efficient and fun.

But no need for fancy websites. Trading was one way to get around the general unpleasantness of the car market, especially if you have someone like me who's willing to do all the work. When I make car trades, I do the hard stuff for the other person. I worry about paperwork and logistics. I arrange shipping and transfer titles. I do all the research. I come up with comps. People are complacent and don't want to do the work. If we trade, all the other person has to do is say thumbs-up or thumbs-down, and the used car taking up space in their driveway disappears or their dream car just shows up at their house.

---

**Inefficient markets with a bad customer experience are good candidates for trading.**

---

I was getting so many messages inquiring about the Mustang that I was having trouble vetting them all. That's why I missed three Instagram messages from Kaitlyn asking if I wanted to trade her for a 2011 Jeep Patriot Sport.

*Hey I was wondering if you would trade your mustang for a 2011 Jeep Patriot sport*, she wrote to me on October 18.

*Meeeee*, she replied to one of my messages on October 19.

*Trade me*, she wrote again.

Then in reply to another story I'd posted saying the Mustang was still available: *Meee!!!!!!*

This time, I finally saw it. *Hi! Whatcha got?* I asked.

THE TRADE ME PROJECT

I'd said I was looking for an RV, so she began by explaining it wasn't an RV, but it was a bigger and nicer car. Then she sent a bunch of pictures of a white Jeep in really nice shape.

I was definitely interested. It was still a car but a nicer one. I sent over my pictures of the Mustang, and we exchanged information on mileage and condition. The Jeep had 145,000 miles on it, which was way less than the Mustang. Kaitlyn didn't care—she just liked the Mustang. There'd been an error on her title, and she had just paid to get it fixed and sent to her. The new title would arrive this week. The timing was perfect, and it seemed like once again, I was getting a way better deal.

## Perception of a Dollar

Trades of higher amounts are actually *easier* to trade up. But why is this? Why is it easier to trade a $1,000 item for a $1,600 item (an increase of $600) but impossible to trade a $10 item for a $610 item (also an increase of $600)? According to Dan Ariely, Professor of Behavioral Economics at Duke University, this is just one feature of irrational economics. People stop being price sensitive over a certain amount.

If you're going to spend $650,000 on a house, you might as well spend $665,000—that seems logical, right? But it isn't. Few people casually spend

> $15,000 more than they meant to. But once we get
> to big numbers, the incremental differences don't
> seem to matter that much compared to the overall
> amount. It's not rational, but it's a common behavior.

However, I was back in complicated logistical territory. Kaitlyn lived in *Pennsylvania*, which feels like the farthest place from Seattle on the map. Back to my old friend, uShip. (I think I might have set the record that year in shipping cars across the country as a private citizen.) I made the arrangements, and the Mustang was picked up and driven thousands of miles to Pennsylvania, where Kaitlyn was waiting. The Mustang would be yet another Trade Me Project item I never physically saw.

I did need some help picking up my new Jeep though. Because leveraging the Project's network had turned out so well last time I needed a car moved, I put out the call again. For this trade, a woman named Shannon and her brother responded. They lived about an hour from Kaitlyn and were willing to drive to Kaitlyn's home to grab the Jeep, bring it to their place, and store it until I could find the next trade. I gratefully agreed.

I'd now been trading for about six months. During that time, I'd been doing my own marketing on social media, and I was starting to get real publicity. Traditional media had gotten wind of the Trade Me Project, and it all snowballed.

I was still managing all my own PR, did tons of interviews, and even began making appearances on daytime TV. Because I was constantly crafting narratives around the Project on TikTok, it came naturally to do the same in interviews.

In addition to traditional media, my follower count on TikTok had reached almost 4.6 million. As my platform continued to grow, it felt like an incredible honor to have so many people on the journey with me, but it also felt like a huge responsibility. The more exposure I got and the larger my audience became, the more imperative it felt I reach my goal—I needed to get that house!

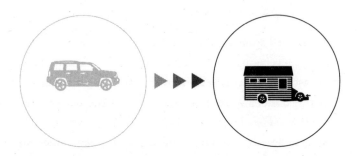

## TRADE 23: 2011 JEEP PATRIOT SPORT FOR A WILDBOUND TINY CABIN

I didn't want to keep trading for cars. I was taking steps up in value, but they were incremental. At this rate, it would take me forever to get the house. I'd wanted an RV or camper to trade for the Mustang before Kaitlyn had come to me with the Jeep. So I got on all the marketplaces, set the location for Pennsylvania so the car wouldn't have to go far, and began looking for something in the category of RV or trailer.

Because it was the pandemic and no one could get on a plane, RVs and trailers were hot items. Their popularity meant the market was inflated and the supply was somewhat limited. But after days of searching, I found something really cool listed in the same city where Shannon lived: a self-described 5- x 8-foot Tiny Cabin manufactured by a company called Wildbound.

The cabin was awesome. It was built on a chassis but looked like a traditional log cabin. Even the size was attractive. Big enough to sleep in but small enough you could literally stick it in your backyard. I loved it, and even though it was a Type B item, I thought I'd definitely be able to find someone who wanted it too.

So, I reached out on Facebook Marketplace, where the tiny cabin was listed. At the time, Facebook Marketplace would only allow you to send the message *Is this still available?* as your opener. I hated this feature because it created a situation where the other person could only respond with a "Yes" or "No" answer. It didn't generate more conversation. Facebook has since removed this limitation, but at the time, it was so frustrating. Trying to close the tiny cabin would be the negotiation of my life.

Once the owner confirmed the tiny cabin was still available, I let them know I had a 2011 Jeep Patriot Sport still under warranty that I was looking to trade. Then I sent a video of the Jeep. The other person was predictably confused.

*You're saying you want to trade the Jeep with me? Or sell the Jeep and buy the cabin?*

I explained I was looking to trade and instantly got shut down. *Not looking for trades.* I was used to that response.

*Ah ok was hoping to trade,* I messaged the cabin's owner and then sent the *Today* article about me and the Trade Me Project. *This is me haha.*

My gamble paid off. The guy on the other end was intrigued. He immediately saw the value of my reach.

*Now on the other hand, 4.6 million followers is a pretty big audience for the business.*

I had done some research as soon as he started responding. I saw that Wildbound was a local company. The avatar of the person responding to me on Facebook looked a lot like the profile picture of the CEO, Austin. He might not want a Jeep, but he'd definitely want the power of the Trade Me Project platform to help advertise his new cabin business.

*Haha definitely. In return for the trade, your company would also be shown to those 4.6M and tagged 👍. Actually the last trade I did where I tagged the company was with an electric bike company and the video got 28M views. ☺*

I had his interest. He asked me if those views were legit. I honestly had no idea how to even buy followers on TikTok, which I told him. He laughed and said he didn't either.

*I was named in the top 50 most viewed creators on TikTok* ☺, I said. Just keeping that conversation going.

*Definitely an impressive following,* he noted.

I explained to him I'd love to work with him on the trade. If he was in, we'd make the exchange and then I'd take care of all the arrangements, including shooting video content I'd edit and post to my socials. We could even tour his operation and show off other cabins.

## Put Yourself in Someone Else's Shoes

Oftentimes, when you have an item you're interested in trading, you must first put yourself in the shoes of the person who'd be interested in trading for it. In doing this, you can ask yourself questions like: "Where would I go if I wanted to buy an item like this?" and "What types of questions would I have about it?" Then, when negotiating, answer those questions before the other person even asks. You can also strategize how and why this item might be useful for someone beyond the obvious use of the item.

Austin was still a little hesitant. It wasn't what he expected, and he was open about that. Would we need to meet up somewhere or …

No, I told him. I didn't see many of the trades at this point. I'd make all the arrangements remotely and Trade Me Project volunteers would help out. He wouldn't have to do anything, and in return, his company would get a tremendous amount of attention.

Austin started brainstorming with me over messages about the best way to promote Wildbound on my social channels. The videos were fairly short—how would we max out eyeballs on it? Was there a way to embed a link to his website so people could immediately click through? He was asking all the right questions, but notice he never once asked about the Jeep. While this would still be a 1:1 trade, it was important that I followed the conversation to where the value was to him.

I made my pitch of all the ways I'd leverage the Trade Me Project platform to amplify Wildbound. TikTok, Instagram, and Instagram Stories would all feature him and the trade. He'd be tagged on all three channels so people would go directly to him. Once we did the trade, I'd make more videos showing the cabin and all its features. Finally, he'd be mentioned in future news articles as one of the Project's trades.

*We can hop on the phone and chat about it more, but I think if you want eyes on your company this is the way to get an easy 1M+.*

He didn't respond. I'd turned on Read Receipts, an essential feature of any digital messaging app, and realized he'd seen my message but had stopped replying right away. I was afraid of losing momentum and giving him too much time to think about it and justify why it was a bad idea.

## The Power of Read Receipts

In the digital world, many messaging apps have the ability to let you see when someone else has read your message. This will allow you to get a glimpse into how the other person is thinking. You can quickly see:

- If a person is reading and replying quickly

- If they're reading and then taking a day to reply

- If they're reading, typing, and deleting their text and then waiting before typing again

In analyzing their typing/reading behaviors, you can understand how close or far a person is in making a trade (or even simply how interested they are in making a trade). Someone who's responding quickly is decisive and eager, while someone who's slow to reply or taking time to craft their responses is either disinterested or playing a game. This way, you know where you stand and how to best respond.

Using Read Receipts is so important. They're a common feature of any digital conversation, but they're also my quickest way of monitoring how a negotiation's going. If someone is reading and responding to my messages right away, we're in good shape. If someone's leaving me on read, that means they're interested but hesitant. If they're straight up ignoring my messages, the trade is dead.

**Use Read Receipts to monitor interest in the trade and control the conversation.**

Managing the cadence and seeing which of my responses get immediate answers is so helpful in controlling the conversation. In this case, I'd done as much as I could via messengers. I needed to keep the conversation going and get to more direct communication.

*What is your cell,* I asked, *I'll shoot you a text so we can get out of messenger haha.*

He responded, and we got on the phone.

**Switch up communication channels when you get stuck.**

Our talk that day was one of many phone conversations we had. Austin was a smart guy with a really interesting product. He understood the value of what the Trade Me Project platform could do for him, but he just wasn't sure about letting go of one of the tiny houses. They were expensive to manufacture, and the sale price of the Jeep wouldn't cover it. The value of the marketing had to make up for that difference.

Giving up isn't really in my DNA, but I thought about it for this one. We were spending a ton of time on the phone, and he just couldn't get there. But—I knew I was so close on the trade. If I could just get him to see how much value the publicity would bring him. At the same time, I couldn't make any promises the PR would directly convert to sales. That was a choice he had to make on his own. All I could do was offer him some guidance and make my best case.

I clearly remember being gathered with my family for Thanksgiving and bailing out on part of dinner to go talk to Austin on the phone. Part of trading is knowing when to give up—and when to *push*. After the Thanksgiving call with Austin, I was exhausted and decided to give Shannon a call to let her know she may need to hold the Jeep a bit longer than expected at her house.

I explained I'd been working all week on a trade with a guy who had a "tiny cabin." In that moment, something clicked.

Shannon—the girl who'd picked up the Jeep and was keeping it for me—knew Austin. They'd gone to high school together. We were shocked. What were the chances that

Shannon and Austin knew each other? Shannon immediately picked up the phone, called Austin, and vouched I was a good person. A few days later, Austin was in.

## Negotiation Tips

- Listen to what the other person wants to understand their motivations.

- Know when to push.

- Know when to back off.

- Use Read Receipts to monitor the ebbs and flows of conversations.

- Find common ground (or common people).

I hadn't exactly gotten the house, but I wanted to create a little excitement after having been quiet for weeks while I was working on this trade. The video I posted announced: *WE DID IT* with two emojis of houses.

In the video, I explained I'd found my next trade in the same town the Jeep was in. Shannon took footage of herself dropping off the Jeep and showing off our brand-new tiny cabin. (I also made sure to explain the Wildbound business and show off all the features of the cabin.) It had a cool rustic aesthetic and was outfitted with a bed, storage, shelving, interior lighting, and a countertop. It was designed to be towed behind a car or truck. I *loved* it.

I finished up my video saying, *While technically it's not the house, it's definitely a step in the right direction.*

Some people in the comments accused me of just doing a sponsored brand deal, but that wasn't the case. Yes, Austin was primarily interested in the Project's platform, but the trade was still an exchange of the Jeep and the Wildbound tiny cabin. Which was now parked at Shannon's in place of the Jeep. Shannon was a saint.

Ironically, though, this is the trade that did end up getting me a brand deal. Fiverr, the digital marketplace for freelance business services, reached out to me. At first, they asked if I would trade with them. No, I told them. I didn't do deals with brands, and I meant that. They came back to me and suggested working together another way. What if they set me up with some kind of freelancer, whose services I could use to enhance the tiny cabin?

It actually wasn't a bad idea. The tiny cabin was beautiful, but it was pretty rustic. The vibe inside was definitely "old summer camp cabin." Adding some touches to the interior might expand the market of who was interested.

Fiverr offered to set me up with Nicole, an interior designer who'd reimagine the interior of the cabin. She came out to see it and did an amazing job. She redid all the textiles on the bed and added wall hangings (which she made), succulents, and a fully kitted-out eating area. It was all-natural fabrics in bright whites and neutral beiges. It looked incredible, like something you'd see on Airbnb in Palm Springs or Byron Bay. While Fiverr was a brand, working with them felt like fixing up the vacuum. I'd used what was available—for free—to make my item more attractive to trade.

That boost was needed because I'd traded for the cabin in November, and it was now *January*. I had been working on the Project since May of 2020, and the end of the first calendar year was closing out. I made a video recapping all my trades in 2020—and even I was surprised by how many I had done. All the way up from a bobby pin to a tiny cabin—with lots of fluctuations and deviations along the way.

Trading had slowed down over the holidays and into the New Year. I hated how long it was taking to find the right trade, but all my moves needed to be smart now. I felt like the house was closer than it had ever been, and I didn't want to go backward anymore.

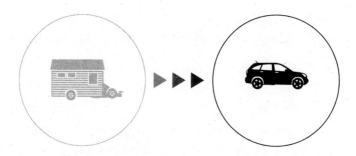

## TRADE 24: WILDBOUND TINY CABIN FOR A HONDA CRV

The tiny cabin was a Type B item for sure. I couldn't just offer it to anyone who had an item I wanted. I needed the right person to come to me. The one interesting bargaining chip I had was there wasn't really anything like it on the market.

---

**The power of being the only item on the market is *you* set the value.**

---

Being the only item on the market can be a powerful thing. With a 2017 MacBook Pro or a 2011 Jeep Patriot, anyone can get online and figure out what the value should be. But what do you charge for a custom Wildbound Tiny Cabin with an interior spruced up by Fiverr?

Who knows really. The value of the cabin was whatever it was worth to the person interested. I could set the price range and see what people did with that information. For some people, it was way too high; for others, it seemed fair.

## You Sometimes Set the Value

Gone are the days when you have to physically go to many stores to compare the value of an item to make sure you're "getting the best deal." Today, people can simply go to Google, Facebook Marketplace, or other digital platforms and compare items and their prices at the tap of a button. In the resale market specifically, users set the prices of their own goods. For items that are already in high supply, it's not advantageous for the seller to make their price much higher than the next person.

For example, if I have a jet ski from 2004 and there are already 30 other identical jet skis on the market for $3,000, then the market's decided what I should price mine at. *But* if there are no jet skis matching those specs currently on the market, I'm able to list mine for $5,000. Without comps, I set the value at whatever I believe a reasonable amount to be. But why is this important for trades? When making a trade, many people will do a quick search to price-check the item. In many cases during the Trade Me Project, I was able to be the only item on the market. Because of this, I was able to set the value and have even more flexibility in influencing the trade.

Of course, being the only custom Wildbound Tiny Cabin on the market also came with challenges. Setting your own value is a double-edged sword. People will be skeptical of whatever you say, and you constantly have to explain what your item is and justify the value.

By now it was February, and I was getting a little desperate. The tiny cabin had been parked at Shannon's house forever. Every time it snowed, she had to go out and shovel it. (As I said, she was really a star and a true friend to the Project.)

Trade after trade after trade fell through. One was in Florida, the next was in California, and the final one was in Georgia. They all backed out. I spent months talking to these people, only to hit dead end after dead end. In total, I sent *2,000* messages trying to get this trade done before I finally worked my way into the trade that landed.

## Test Your Replies

In sending hundreds of thousands of messages, I've begun to A/B test my replies. This means I test out different type of replies to understand which will get the highest percent of replies. For example, if I were to send a message that said "Are you interested in trading your boat for my car?" I might get a 15% reply rate. But if I send a message that says "Great! I have a Ford Escape with only 100K miles and no issues that I'd love to trade for the boat," that might get an 80% response rate. As you learn which replies garner the most responses, continue to use the one that performs best—or continue to tweak until you're happy with your response rate.

Finally—*finally*—the right person saw my Stories about the cabin. Again, having the Trade Me Project's platform was a blessing and a curse. Even though I was spending at least six hours a day actively trying to make trades, I still didn't have enough time to read all the messages I got. That sometimes meant I missed important ones.

Katie lived in Arizona, and she was offering me a 2008 Honda CRV. It had 141,000 miles on it and the photos looked solid. I quickly got us out of messages and onto the phone. I usually want as much information as possible before making a trade, but for this trade, I was nervous to ask her why she wanted the cabin. I was truly worried that one too many questions might scare her off from making the trade. This trade *had* to get done.

Except for a couple fun videos, I'd been silent on TikTok for months—and people were getting impatient.

Ultimately, the trade went through and the cabin made its way across the United States from Pennsylvania to Phoenix, where Katie handed over the keys and title to her Honda CRV. To thank Shannon, who'd gone above and beyond, I decided it would be only fitting to feature her in her own

Trade Me Project TikTok video. The truth is, over the months that Shannon had the tiny cabin, we spoke on the phone a ton and became good friends.

During one of our many calls, she explained she'd been trying to save $7,000 within a year to pay off her student loans. She was working two jobs, and paying off the loans would be a huge step. That comment stuck in my mind for weeks.

When I finally made the video, I explained who Shannon was and how much she'd helped the project, and I shared her goal of hitting $7,000. Within just a few days, she was halfway to her goal, and within a month, she'd hit it—all because of incredible donations from Trade Me Project followers.

I also later got my answer to why Katie wanted the tiny cabin: She was converting it into an outdoor bar in her backyard for the pandemic. Incredible.

I was so relieved to be out of Type B items and back into a Type A item that had broad appeal and a discernible price point. I was always going back and forth between the two categories. I'd get burned out on Type A trading strategies and then try Type B again. Those would be more complex and fun, but they also tended to take forever. Back to Type A. And so on.

The only problem was that the Honda CRV had some cosmetic issues—a few scratches and a big dent. This is when another brand deal came my way. AutoZone reached out wanting to trade me something. No, I couldn't trade with brands, but my experience with Fiverr taught me there were other ways to leverage those relationships to create value for both of us. How about they help me fix up the car?

AutoZone did an incredible job of not only helping me with some basic maintenance but also sending the car to the Scottsdale Collision Center, where they put in a ton of work getting the dent out and detailing the car. I couldn't believe the transformation. As I noted in the video I made, the car looked absolutely brand new.

One part of the Trade Me Project I don't often talk about is the brand deal side—not because I don't want to talk about it but because it feels like a distraction from getting back to the trades. What *is* interesting is that the hustle and determination I felt while making and finding trades was the same determination I felt while finding brands to work with.

For the first year and a half of the Trade Me Project, I was managing all the brands on my own. While I did eventually get an agent, I never felt like they really understood me. I knew my craft best. The most important part for me was making sure the brand was something I actually needed or used during the Trade Me Project. Maybe AutoZone wasn't as sexy as hair care gummies (no disrespect!), but they were legitimately an amazing partner to me during my trades.

Just like the Trade Me Project in general, I think people, even agents, underestimated how determined I'd be to land deals that made sense for the Project. I cold-called and emailed hundreds of brands I used and loved during the Project. I crafted and sent my own pitch. Once I got a reply,

I'd get on a video call and try to immediately read what kind of brand they were and what specifically I could bring to the table that they didn't have.

I could sometimes tell it was a brand that was new to TikTok, in which case I'd pitch that I could help be their "entrance into TikTok." Other times, the brand wanted to drive sign-ups to their website or downloads to their app. I had different strategies for each brand I eventually worked with. After we hung up, I'd then send a proposal uniquely catered to what I'd gleaned from the call. Most times, they were interested.

Eventually, my brand deals picked up momentum. In the time I'd landed 10 brand deals, my agent had maybe landed one. No shame to them—I just knew myself better than anyone else. To this day, I feel like I can pitch anyone on anything. My pitches became crystal clear.

At some point, there was a brand (which I won't name) that after the video I did with them went live joked they got more views from my single video than they did during the Super Bowl. I wasn't even shocked because I knew what I was doing. I'd spent so, so many hours learning the business of the Trade Me Project that I could handle that aspect of it on my own. At that point, I didn't need an agent. I was my own agent, scheduler, designer, and more—with Bobby's unwavering help and support, of course.

Just to be clear because this is so important to me: Even though I was making good money on brand deals, I still never spent money to fix up a trade or took money in exchange for a trade. I was dead set that I was going to do this Project according to the rules I'd created. At one point, I had a woman pick up a trade for me, and she mentioned the car (the trade) was really dirty and that I should probably take it to the car wash if I wanted a chance at trading it. I explained to her I couldn't spend a penny and that even if no one ever found out, I didn't want to break my three trading rules.

A caveat: The one rule about money I did have, as you've probably noticed, is I could spend money on *shipping*. As the items I was trading for became larger, it just felt wrong to find a trade with someone and then say, "Awesome, thanks for the trade, but you have to pay to ship my end of the trade and yours." That's a bad deal for them, and I didn't believe in making deals that weren't good for the other person.

Throughout the Project, I stayed true to my rules and only paid for shipping costs. That sometimes meant paying for a car to be shipped 20 minutes away or that sometimes meant paying for three tractors to be shipped all the way across the country (spoiler). Costs ranged from a couple hundred dollars to a couple thousand.

To be totally transparent: My most expensive shipping cost was shipping the tiny cabin on wheels from Harleysville, Pennsylvania, to Scottsdale, Arizona. The trip was 2,342 miles and cost $2,500. Remember, not all trades had to be shipped. Some were local or drivable enough that I could get them there myself or with the help of others.

I probably spent around $8,000 on shipping costs for the Project in total, but that felt okay given that the end result would be a house worth at least $100,000. (Plus, the money used on shipping was coming directly from the brand deals I was landing with the help of the Trade Me Project.) I never wanted the shipping to be the limiting factor of why I didn't make a trade. Honestly, I believe I could still do it without shipping. (Maybe that's a rule for Season 3!)

Back to the CRV, I was worried that the long breaks in posting would mean people lost interest, but the opposite was true. The comments on my video about getting the CRV fixed couldn't have been nicer. Having a few high-value trades in a row created a perception of true momentum. No more stationary bikes. No more used computers. No more vacuums. I was solidly in the high-value end of trading. People were *so* excited and truly believed the house would happen. It was their faith and enthusiasm that kept pushing me.

**syd:** *THIS HAS COME SO FAR.* [14.6K likes]

**mattloveshair:** *LETS GET THIS HOUSE!!!*

**Austin:** *You are doing so incredible. This is unreal.*

**User652903566929:** *The progress you've made is ridiculous*

It was a good thing people were so invested because I had my sight set on a particular item. I'd seen it on YouTube, and

I wanted it—bad. I was throwing everything I could at the wall to make the trade stick, and I was sure it would hype up my followers even more. Once I pulled it off, I couldn't wait to share, but little did I know, it would end up being the most controversial trade in the history of the Project.

# CHAPTER 10

# THE MOST CONTROVERSIAL TRADE IN THE WORLD

One day I was scrolling the Internet, and I saw an article about something called the Chipotle Celebrity Card. I can't remember who the article was about, but I was so intrigued. What was this thing?

The Chipotle Celebrity Card was an ultra-exclusive, invite-only program that had been created in 2003. The program was started because of Ozzy Osbourne's love for Chipotle, which he spoke about very publicly on his reality show. To reward him and keep the free promotion going, Chipotle created a card that entitled him to a year of free Chipotle.

This card let you eat for free at Chipotle and included a catered dinner for 50 people. No amount of money could buy you one. You had to be someone famous, like a musician or actor, or become famous for your love for Chipotle.

"To be considered for a Celebrity Card, you must be an authentic fan of Chipotle and organically be sharing your passion for the brand in everyday life," said Candice Beck, director of social and influencers at Chipotle (what a job).

I wanted one.

When I saw the card, I began reaching out to Chipotle to ask if we could do a trade. Right—I do remember I said I don't trade with brands, and that's true. But this wasn't a brand deal. I wasn't making a gimmicky trade by giving them the car for a burrito or something. Chipotle had something that wasn't available for purchase. The only way to get one was to be offered it—or to trade for it if they were willing. (And this would be a trade offer.)

I didn't know anyone at Chipotle or have an agent who could figure out who to talk to there. I just started reaching out to Chipotle via my social channels and also messaging anyone relevant on LinkedIn who worked at the company. Sometimes, to get to the right person, you have to be willing to do a lot of swinging and missing. The worst thing that can happen is someone says "No" (and maybe blocks you).

I did finally find my way to the right people at Chipotle. They took note of the Trade Me Project's platform and were intrigued. They understood my pitch and agreed that making a trade could be the perfect match between the Project and the intended use of their celebrity card. Did they want a Honda CRV? Absolutely not.

I got it. The Honda wasn't useful to them at all and didn't match their brand messaging. I started offering them everything I could think of and reasons they'd want it. A van? A bus? An industrial-sized ice cream maker? (I knew where to get one of those!) A tractor?

*Sure!* they said, *a tractor sounds great!*

*Amazing,* I said, *because I'm working on a trade for one now.*

Lies. I had zero tractors in the trade pipeline. I didn't even know where I'd start looking for a tractor (definitely not in San Francisco!). I frantically started trying to track one down.

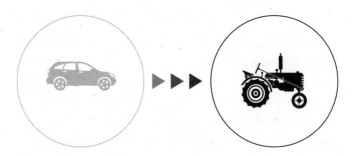

## TRADE 25: HONDA CRV FOR THREE TRACTORS

What I was doing here was something I'd do a few more times in the Project: I was making a leapfrog trade. I'd identified an item I wanted, but I didn't have what the other person wanted. I needed to go get something they did want by making one—or more—trades with my existing item.

---

**Your path won't always be direct, so make intermediary leapfrog trades to get to your goal.**

---

I went back to my old buddy, Facebook Groups. I joined possibly every tractor Facebook Group in America. (There are more than you'd think.) I offered everyone and their mother my Honda CRV, but for a while, it just wasn't happening. (By "a while," I mean months.) I started working on the trade in early February and I wouldn't land my tractors until the end of April.

Eventually, I found not one, not two, but *three* tractors their owner was willing to trade. The tractors were older—from 1940—so they were really more antiques than useful equipment. They were painted a bright red and were valued at $3,700 each for a total of $11,100. They were being kept on a property in Oregon, so I'd once again have to arrange shipping. Honestly, at this point, the logistics were the easiest part of this whole thing.

## Never Trade for Multiple Items

While on paper it might sound great to be able to trade one item and get two or three items in return, these trades are actually much harder to get rid of. Why is that? It's already hard enough to find someone who's interested in the one item you have, but it's even harder to find someone who's interested in two or more different items to justify the full value. This rule can be ignored if the item is something that would typically be sold in pairs or together (e.g., a tennis racket and balls) or if the items are the same (e.g., a pair of jet skis). It's especially an exception when Chipotle wants three tractors for their Celebrity Card.

Before okaying the trade, I went back to Chipotle to make sure these tractors were something they'd want. This is a key step in leapfrog trades. The intermediary trades need sign-off from the goal trade; otherwise, you've wasted your time.

Chipotle was into it. They have a pretty serious program partnering with farmers in their supply chain, and the tractors could have some cool use there. Either they'd let farmers actually use them or they could keep them at their headquarters as décor. The trade made sense for their brand and got me the thing I'd been dreaming about: a Chipotle Celebrity Card.

Having their sign-off made the logistics a little simpler. Instead of shipping the tractors from Oregon to my place in San Francisco, where I'd literally never be able to store them (remember the parking situation with the van?), the tractors could go right to Los Angeles near Chipotle headquarters. They couldn't assume ownership until we made the trade, so I arranged for the tractors to be shipped to a storage unit near their office building. Then I had a reality check and it hit me: I was going to ship *three tractors* hundreds of miles to a self-storage facility in LA. Was I *insane?!?*

Guess so because that's exactly what I did. I had someone from uShip grab the Honda CRV from Phoenix and bring it up to Oregon. Then the three—*three!*—tractors were put on a truck and hauled down to Los Angeles to their new home in storage. My new friends at Chipotle were there to receive them and get them in the unit because I couldn't be there that day. Unfortunately, no one could figure out how to get the

tractors to start. I was literally on FaceTime with the driver
from uShip googling "how to start a tractor." Eventually, they
got enough people to just haul the tractors into the unit
without turning them on. That's one way to
do it.

I arranged to head down to LA the following week, where
I'd finally see the tractors in person and film the trade reveal.
First, I got footage of the tractors being transported and then
filmed myself opening up the storage unit. When I posted the
video to TikTok, the official Chipotle account left a comment:

**Chipotle:** 👀

… and I responded back:

**Trademeproject:** *Oh hey* 👋👋

My next trade was on.

## TRADE 26: THREE TRACTORS FOR A CHIPOTLE CELEBRITY CARD

Seeing the tractors in person was wild. They were *huge*. Now that I was here, I needed to figure out how to turn them on so we could move them wherever Chipotle wanted them to go. Bobby and I have so much B-roll footage of me trying to get the tractors started. I did finally get them on, so we also have tons of footage of me learning (i.e., googling and teaching myself) how to drive them. When I attempted to back the first one out of the unit, it jerked backward and I almost shot out of the seat. By the time I drove out the third one, I was a pro.

Jacob, who's part of Chipotle's farming partnership program, met me at the storage units. We filmed him handing over the celebrity card, which comes in its own "custom Baltic birch plywood box" with a cool design etched on the top. But the best part was—this trade was unbuyable. That made the trade seem invaluable to me. I was so excited to post the video and share. To me, this was the biggest trade I'd made to date.

I had no idea what was coming for me.

As soon as I posted the video, comments started rolling in. Instead of being excited, people straight up *hated* this trade— and they weren't shy about telling me. I won't name usernames, but I got thousands of comments like this:

*Girl you just took 3,000 steps back.*

*For a year … girl go get your tractor back.*

*feels like ur going downhill*

*This is such a bad trade*

*She went from a car to a gift card* 😒

*Tell me you got scammed without telling me you got scammed*

*U traded 3,000 dollars for 300 dollars*

*Worst trade ever, this is obviously a sponsored vid w/ chipotle, and the card wasn't the only thing you got!*

*Nahhhhhh what* 💀

*No thats THE WORST TRADE YOU'VE EVER DONE*

I was totally unprepared.

It was probably even worse because, unlike the Peloton or the Boosted Board—where I knew I had made a down trade and expected some disappointment—I honestly thought I'd crushed it. The trade was real, and it was for something I thought was so cool. A Celebrity Card isn't a gift card. You could use the card every day. You could buy food for the person next to you in line or for the homeless person outside! Why wouldn't you use it that way? That was worth way more than $300.

But people didn't see it that way. And on the Internet, people love to hate.

I got so many comments that I did something I never thought I'd have to do. I recorded a video titled "My Latest Trade" and explained I'd gotten some pretty wild comments. I said I was human; I read every single comment and had to turn them off because they were so painful to read. Also, I gave my followers some insight into my thought process behind the trade—why I'd thought it was such a good deal. People could go in and buy burritos every day for themselves, their family and friends, or as random acts of kindness. With the catered dinner, I priced that at $18,000.

It was tough, but I knew I would keep pushing through. I finished up with my usual sign-off: Let's get that house.

The comments on this video weren't really any better. People were *harsh*. Of course, some people came to my defense and were supportive, which I appreciate to this day, but I still got tons of flak. While my digital platform had been such a cool part of this experience, it wasn't the core of it. The trades were what mattered. I decided to refocus my energy there. Once I had the house, I'd prove all the haters wrong.

With a little more distance, it's easier for me to diagnose why the Chipotle Celebrity Card provoked such a strong reaction. Even though I didn't view this as a brand deal in the traditional sense, I think the fact I traded with a brand made people suspicious. People loved how authentic the Trade Me Project felt. I was so grateful for the ways in which people were rooting for me, but that focus on authenticity also meant there was a fair amount of scrutiny. I wish people had known I took the self-imposed rules of the Project way more seriously than they did.

In addition, if I'd traded with a brand for an item that people understood better, I don't think I'd have gotten the backlash. For example, if it had been a vehicle or a luxury item that was more tangible for people to grasp, I might have been okay. But the combination of the brand and the card was what sunk me. Although, like I said, I'm still surprised. I genuinely thought the Chipotle Celebrity Card was a great trade.

Worth at least three antique tractors—no question.

## TRADE 27: CHIPOTLE CELEBRITY CARD FOR AN OFF-THE-GRID TRAILER

The best revenge would have been trading the Chipotle Celebrity Card right away, ideally for a house. But that didn't happen. The next trade wouldn't happen quickly, and there were a few reasons why I got stuck. I did eventually unblock myself, but it took a lot of work.

The biggest problem I faced with my Chipotle card was there was a serious mismatch between who wanted the card and who could "afford" it. Just like the sneakers and the Mustang, I'd accidentally found myself solidly in a market where the demand was dominated by ... teenagers. The same week I traded for the card, a prominent YouTuber was given one (Addison Rae, whose card was hand-delivered by Tony Hawk), and Gen Z freaked out. Their reaction made me feel like this was a great idea. Little did I know, only teenagers agreed with me.

That mismatch between the demographic and the items they had to trade killed me. I got message after message from teenagers begging me for the card and offering whatever they had—their video game systems, their old computers, their iPhones. They'd sometimes offer me multiple things, which is never a good idea. (Trades should be 1:1—unless it's three tractors. Obviously.)

So I had an unexpectedly Type B item, which usually requires mass marketing and then waiting for inbound interest. That process was broken this time, though, because all the inbound interest wasn't qualified.

Trying to proactively locate the right person for a Type B item is difficult, but it can be done. Using the Internet to locate fans is one good strategy. For example, joining fan groups for sneakers and then messaging the actual followers or commenters of those accounts is one way to go about it. Maybe I could do the same thing with Chipotle.

Using a few different analytics sites, I combed through Chipotle's Twitter page and made a list of all the verified accounts that tweet at them. Then I messaged those people directly. Similarly, I got on Chipotle fan groups on Facebook and Instagram. I reached out to the people who'd also joined those pages.

I really thought this would work, but I was striking out. Because the trade was taking so long, I posted some filler videos using current trends. The Chipotle Celebrity Card backlash continued. People left comment after comment telling me how dumb my trade was and predicting that the Trade Me Project was over. It was super uplifting.

I did make another "how to" video titled: *How to start your own Trade Me Project journey.* I was officially at the one-year mark of the Trade Me Project, and the best way to celebrate would be to kick people off on their own trades.

Trading wasn't and isn't the easiest hobby, but it's also been so fulfilling. Even though I was currently stuck with a Chipotle Celebrity Card, I knew my next trade would happen—even if a large portion of the Internet disagreed with me.

I took a little time off from trading and secretly moved to Europe for the summer. Bobby and I were able to work remotely, and our dog, Earl, travels well. We rented a place in Copenhagen and spent the summer riding our bikes, drinking wine, and just generally having an amazing time. I'd been so focused on doing nothing but working my tech job and running the Trade Me Project that a change of pace felt incredible.

**Trading is hard—and tuning out the haters is key.**

Of course, I was still logging into all my apps, sending my outbound messages, and doing everything I could to get someone to trade me something amazing for the Chipotle Card. When things look bleak, this is always when the magic of trading kicks in.

Then, of all things, I get a random email.

I almost didn't open the email. It came to my Trade Me Project email account, which might get inbound press interest—but that's it. Inbound trade interest comes through TikTok, Facebook, Instagram, and sometimes even LinkedIn. All my social channels. But email? It had never happened to me before.

The email was also super professional. It was from a woman named Alyssa. Alyssa lived in Vancouver, Canada, where she had her own sustainable flower company, Leis de Buds (pronounced like "lady buds"). She explained she didn't watch my videos, but one of her employees did. During the pandemic, she'd bought a trailer and converted it into a mobile florist shop. She and her team were able to roll up anywhere and create beautiful arrangements with their organically grown flowers.

However, since the pandemic was winding down and they were back in their normal space, she no longer needed the trailer—and she really liked Chipotle. She wasn't necessarily a Chipotle superfan, but she laid out her case for how she could use the card: feeding her employees or the clients at the women's shelter where she volunteered. The card could be useful in all these different facets of her life. This made me so happy. In the back of my mind, I was always hoping someone would use the card to do something charitable, not just eat Chipotle in their homes.

The email was so clear and professional. It was totally different from the random DMs I was used to. I did some sleuthing, checking out her website and LinkedIn. *I have to get her on the phone*, I thought. She was a businesswoman; she'd be used to negotiating a deal live rather than going back and forth over email.

I emailed Alyssa back and we set up a time to talk. When we got on the phone, I realized something important: She wasn't sold on the trade.

Yes, she'd reached out to me—and she was interested. But this was not a done deal, as I'd assumed it was after reading her email. She was opening up a conversation, not coming to me ready to pick up a Chipotle Celebrity Card and offload her trailer. I was going to have to sell the card and her participation in the Project.

Just like with Austin, the owner of the Wildbound Tiny Cabins, when the trade has a business element, it's really important to get off social media messaging apps and talk live. It would be like trying to close a deal over text—that's much harder than talking through the negotiation in real time. Once I was serious about a trade, I always asked if the other person was willing to chat over FaceTime or the phone.

Alyssa and I talked a ton. We got to know each other better, spending time talking about her business (which was such a cool idea) as well as her other goals. For example, she wanted to start a charitable organization. I explained how my platform could help her market not only Leis de Buds, her flower business, but also this other nonprofit idea she had. Beyond that, figuring out how to transport her trailer would be a pain, and I would take care of all that for her ...

Wait, I was going to ship a full-sized, off-the-grid trailer *out of Canada*?

# CHAPTER 11

# LET'S GET THIS HOUSE!

I was. I was going to trade for an off-the-grid trailer that was all the way across the border in Canada and then figure out how to get it into the States. In the middle of a pandemic.

The Trade Me Project had seen some challenges, but this one would require serious effort, brainpower, and teamwork to solve.

I really had no choice. The Chipotle Celebrity Card was still one of my favorite trades, but it had been more than two months since I'd gotten it. I needed to make a move—

any move. And this was a good trade! Unlike the other times when I'd gotten stuck with a Type B item and got myself unblocked by down trading, this wasn't even a down trade! The trailer was amazing. It was valued at $40,000. *$40,000!* If getting a $40,000 trailer into the United States was going to require a little elbow grease, I was more than willing.

I started doing my research, and the little information I could dig up indicated that transporting the trailer across the border was going to be … very difficult. I had no idea how I was going to get this thing, but I was going to figure it out. I always did. If the Trade Me Project has taught me anything, it's that when you have a big goal (like trading a bobby pin for a house), you have to break it down one step at a time.

---

**Like anything in life, to solve big trade problems, approach it one step at a time.**

---

I started by calling the manufacturer of the trailer, Hummingbird, figuring they'd have some experience importing their trailers into the States. As it turned out, they didn't export the trailers themselves, but they had a "guy" who could at least move it and gave me his number. I called him, and he was helpful. He could store the trailer for me at his house and introduced me to the next person who'd be key to this operation—the exporter—who was in charge of the administrative aspects of getting it across the border.

After the exporter and I talked, he went and got all the paperwork together for me and made some recommendations for shippers. It felt like we were on track.

Then we hit our first roadblock. As the exporter was filing the paperwork, he let me know he couldn't export the trailer because the trailer was illegal.

Illegal?

*What?*

I had no idea what he meant. He explained that the structure was okay, but it was the trailer—the platform, hitch, and wheels the mini-house sat on—that was the problem. There was something off about the paperwork that meant no trailer of this type could be imported into the United States. I didn't get it at all, but it sounded like a problem. A serious problem. He recommended I call the trailer platform's manufacturer, which I promptly did.

Or at least I tried to. Their number wasn't listed publicly online. The one number I could find was for the platform manufacturer's warehouse. I called them, and they didn't know how to help me, but they did give me the office number (actually very helpful!).

"Okay, we'll look into it," they told me.

And I waited.

I started calling once a week to check the status of the illegal trailer platform. They weren't sure what was going on either, and they needed the help of *the United States government* to find out. They had to file an official request with the United States Department of Transportation (DOT) to investigate why their trailer system was illegal in the States.

This was getting very complicated.

When the platform manufacturer finally heard back, the DOT told them they had expired paperwork from 2015 when they'd originally registered the trailer system. They needed to refile the paperwork and pay some dues to rectify being out of compliance.

"Great!" I said, thinking the problem was solved.

No, not even close. They could do all the above, but it would take a very long time to go through the approvals process. They had to wait for the DOT to review their case, and even if they paid the dues, there was no guarantee they'd be accepted. At best, this would be wrapped up in two months' time, and it wasn't guaranteed to go my way.

But it probably would. Right?

By that time, I was already committed. If broken-down vans and overvalued diamond necklaces and a mountain of Internet hate hadn't defeated me, then some bureaucratic paperwork issue with the DOT wasn't going to stop me. Plus, by this time, the trade had been made, and one of the golden rules of trading is that once you made a trade, you can't trade back.

This was by far my most complicated trade yet. It was easy to get lost in the layers of complexity. There were five key relationships I was managing here: the person I'd traded with (Alyssa), the trailer manufacturer (Hummingbird), the mover, the exporter, and the platform's manufacturer. I had to keep my eye on all of them while pushing the ball forward. There were so many moves I needed to make to unblock myself, but the most important one was getting the trailer platform legal. The rest I could deal with later.

Feeling like we were close enough, I made a video announcing the trade with the Chipotle Celebrity Card and the off-the-grid trailer. For all the hate I'd been getting, it was so nice to see followers who hadn't lost faith. Tons of people replied, celebrating and saying they'd been sure I could do it. One of the comments I got (and still get) most on my accounts was that someone had been watching from the beginning and was committed to seeing this through with me. I still love it whenever I hear that. It makes me feel like we were in it together. When I said *Let's get that house* (as in *all of us together*), I meant it.

Showing off the trailer was super gratifying after months of digital bullying. The trailer was amazing. It had a giant walk-in fridge (perfect for all of Alyssa's flowers) as well as a desk and several large windows. Best of all, it was completely self-sufficient. The entire electrical system, the fridge, and all the outlets were run completely by a giant Tesla Powerwall 2 and solar panels. I envisioned someone using it as a backyard office, an off-the-grid bitcoin mining space, or even as a camper (with a really nice fridge). This is exactly what I said in my video. Unlike the last trade, people immediately got the vision. Thank goodness.

The trade was announced, but I still wasn't exactly sure if I could move the trailer across the border yet.

The trailer manufacturer's mover "guy," who'd been so helpful storing the trailer and explaining shipping, had gone fully MIA. I'd arranged for the trailer to be moved from Alyssa's to his house, which happened, and then he totally went dark. I panicked. Had I really come this far to lose everything because I'd trusted the wrong person? The Trade Me Project had been built on the healthy, well-qualified trust of strangers. How ironic if that was its undoing.

I sent approximately one million messages.

Finally—*finally*—I heard back from the guy.

*I'm on the other side of Canada,* he wrote me, *I bought a school and I'm making it into a house and—*

*Okay, cool—but WHERE IS THE TRAILER,* I thought. Tempting—but instead, I typed: *Cool! Where's the trailer?*

*Oh, it's at my house still with my ex-wife,* he said, *but I don't have the keys …*

*Okay, where did the keys go?* I asked him.

He didn't know. Then he was missing the title *and* the keys. Was I being scammed or was he just incredibly disorganized? I wasn't willing to find out.

I hired another moving company. I had to get the trailer away from this guy in case he misplaced the entire thing, but the problem was I had nowhere to put it. Even worse, the paperwork *still* wasn't ready. I couldn't move it across the border, but I couldn't leave it with my well-intentioned but squirrelly mover friend.

Time to leverage the power of the Trade Me Project network once again. I put out a call on Instagram, following up on my TikTok, asking if there was anyone who lived near the Canadian border between Vancouver and Seattle who would be willing to help me with my trade. This awesome couple responded and said they were two miles from the border. I asked if they were willing to store the trailer for the time being and they agreed.

There was one more hiccup before I got the trailer safely to the couple who were helping me out. The day movers were supposed to arrive, no one was at the guy's house. The title and keys were somewhere inside, and I had no way to get them. I had to scramble to show proof to the moving company that the trailer was really mine and that I hadn't hired them to steal it. Fortunately, I was able to show proof of ownership, and the movers didn't need the keys to hook it up to anything (those were just for getting inside the trailer).

Mission accomplished.

I arranged to visit the couple to come see the trailer and retrieve the title and keys myself. While I was doing all this, I'd also put together a few brand deals in the months I'd spent trying to make trades. Actually, I'd made a TikTok video following a trend, saying: "When you need brands to make distractions in the comments … because your next trade is taking longer than expected." It got incredible results—many, many brands left comments:

**Duolingo:** *don't even have time for dinner over here*

**Trademeproject:** *Better be getting overtime* 👏

**BuzzFeed:** *Ok comment chain below. What's your unpopular opinion?*

**Trademeproject:** *Fun fact: Who knew that I used to work @ BuzzFeed*

(This is true.)

**Windows:** *Is that Rover?*

(My dog was in the video.)

**Trademeproject:** *Ma'am, that's Earl.*

**ADT:** *fashionably late because we were helping protect that pup … whats shakin*

**Trademeproject:** *Protect Earl at all costs* 🗼

**Gopro:** *I'm officially here*

**Trademeproject:** *Seems official enough* 😄

**Taskrabbit:** *Here to help!* 🖤

**Trademeproject:** *But actually, might need your help!*

There were so many more: Domino's, Floor Stuff, Rob's Popcorn, Camping World, My Protein, the American Museum of Natural History (cool!), Flavortown (help), Nerf, Frontier Airlines, Tabasco, and someone pretending to be Crocs. I'll never stop being surprised by the ability of the Internet to make connections, even if it's with the Duolingo owl at 3 in the morning.

One outcome of this random exercise was that I landed a deal with Volkswagen. They partnered with me to let me borrow a Volkswagen Taos SEL for the road trip. It was a flashy, bright blue SUV, and I loved driving it. The partnership made sense because I needed to go visit the trailer in Canada, and my only form of transportation was a bike. Bobby and I loaded up the borrowed Volkswagen and made the 15-hour drive north.

Seeing the trailer in person was *so* exciting. For most of the other large items, like the tiny cabin or the many cars, I'd never seen them live before or after they were traded. Sure, I had plenty of photos and videos, but actually getting to see it for myself was a totally different experience. I'd gone from a bobby pin to—*this!* The trailer was huge, fancy, and so cool. Seeing it in person made it feel so real and yet the moment was totally surreal. We'd come so far.

I put together another brand deal with Fiverr, the company I'd worked with on the tiny cabin. I was planning on sprucing up the trailer anyway, and they helped me design and laser-cut a cool Trade Me Project logo to put on the side of the new trailer. Bobby and I had rolled up to the trailer with some cans of paint and basic DIY supplies only to find it was literally 13 feet tall. There was no way we'd brought enough paint to cover even one side of it.

The trailer didn't even really need improvements—it looked great. But I'd felt so antsy just working on paperwork all those months that I wanted to do *something*. Still, we went out and got more paint and then gave it a fresh coat. (This time with the help of a professional painter.) I also thought I might as well test all the appliances and systems while I was there. This was smart because we couldn't get the Tesla battery working. I was googling and calling Alyssa to ask for advice. After working on it for a couple hours, we finally got it going.

The trailer was ready. Now the paperwork the trailer platform manufacturer was refiling needed to be finished so

I could have the exporter refile the paperwork to get it across the border—and hire a new (reliable) mover who'd actually handle the logistics. Managing all these different relationships and getting unblocked at every turn had been exhausting, but I knew I was close.

I'd been working with the trailer platform manufacturer for several months to get the new paperwork done. I called them at least once a week—often more—and they knew my name and number. The person handling the paperwork and I would catch up and discuss how it was going. I'm sure they were sick of me by the end, but I really appreciated their efforts.

In amazing timing, during the road trip to Canada, I got the final call: The paperwork had been accepted. Waiting those two extra months had been worth it. The off-the-grid trailer, including the platform it rested on, was now totally legal and ready to cross the border.

Usually, people hire third-party services to help with import/export, but these services are *expensive*. The Trade Me Project had been built on the kindness of strangers and my willingness to do anything and everything myself. Little did I know, a year and a half earlier, when I was rubbing scuffs off a vacuum, that the skills I'd eventually need to acquire would get way crazier before this thing was done.

Once the trailer was officially legal, I handled all the rest of the import paperwork myself. I filed all the paperwork with an imports/exports board and found someone willing to tow the trailer. The driver picked up the trailer from the lovely couple near the border, who'd been such rock stars, and started driving.

*I won't have signal when I do the crossing,* the driver texted me.

*No problem,* I told him, *I'll wait.* I was so incredibly nervous. I'd spent months putting all the pieces in place, and I'd never imported a vehicle into the country before.

What if it all went wrong?!?

*I'm being called inside the building,* he messaged me, and then went dead.

*Oh my god,* I thought.

A few minutes later, I got a call from him.

"We have a problem," he said.

My heart sank.

"The bill of sale wasn't signed, so they won't let me drive it into the country."

That was wrong—I knew the bill of sale had been signed by Alyssa, and I'd checked it. I scrambled to get on my computer and start going through all my thick files of paperwork. When I looked at the attachments I'd emailed him, I realized I had given him the wrong version of the bill of sale; the one I sent was indeed unsigned.

Desperately hoping this would work, I took a screenshot of the signed PDF and texted it to his phone. He then went to show it to the border agents.

The minutes ticked by.

Was he able to show it?

Did he cross the border?

Did it work?

More time passed.

*You make it?* I texted him, and the message didn't go through. He'd lost signal again.

My heart was racing. I'd spent the last three and a half months preparing for this moment. Was it really a no go because of one signature page?

*Ping* His text came through: *It's over.*

I could have cried. How had it all fallen apart? Was this trade *ever* going to work?

In typical Demi fashion, I pulled it together and immediately went to work restrategizing. I was frantically texting him ideas about what we could do.

*NO*, he wrote back, *it's over the* border*!*

The miscommunication was suddenly clear.

He texted: *It's over.*

He meant: *It's over the border.*

I read: *We can't do this and it's all over.*

He then sent a photo of him and the trailer stateside. I was the most relieved I've felt during the entire Trade Me Project.

In sharing my experience importing a semi-legal trailer into the United States from Canada, I've tried to think about what would be useful takeaways for someone also interested in trading. All I can say is: I hope you never find yourself in this situation.

If you do, do your research, follow up weekly, and double-check all your documents. Or maybe find something less complicated and spare yourself the grief.

The driver and the off-the-grid trailer were over the border, in the States, and on its way to its final location. That's right— its final location. I wasn't moving the trailer to another holding spot in Seattle or wherever before I could make my next trade and figure out its final destination. I knew exactly where the trailer was going. Because I had a secret. A house-shaped secret.

# CHAPTER 12

# LET'S GIVE THIS HOUSE AWAY!

Halfway through the Trade Me Project, I got a random TikTok comment that said *I know someone who may be interested in trading you the house*, and I ignored it because 1) I get so many comments, and 2) I've learned not to trust the ones that look too good to be true.

Then this person reached out to me on another social media platform, telling me again they knew someone who might trade me a house and told me to reach out to Ciera, including her last name. I replied and got a phone number. The whole thing felt really cryptic to me. Who was this mysterious person who traded houses?

I took the phone number and texted this Ciera person.

*Hey, I heard from someone you may be interested in a house trade.*

She was. We got on the phone right away. She explained she was a house flipper and always has a bunch of houses she's working on. Ciera was also really interested in the Trade Me Project journey. While she didn't want whatever small, low-value item I had right now, if I had something cool in the future, she might be interested in trading me. For a house.

I remained skeptical. An entire house? I didn't know if this was legit, but I kept her offer in my back pocket, thinking that maybe in the end, if I had something valuable enough, she could be someone I reach out to. Even though nothing was for certain, I saved her in my phone as "Final House Lady." It felt like a good sign.

---

**Stay connected to people who are open to trading—they might be right for a trade at a later date.**

---

For months, we didn't talk. I knew she was following along with the story based on her views, so I would sporadically reach out just to touch base and see if she was interested in whatever I had at the time. The Chipotle Celebrity Card wasn't good enough. None of the cars were good enough. But eventually, if I had something big enough, I could keep reaching out.

The other thing I knew about her was that she was in a small town in Tennessee called Clarksville, where housing prices are more affordable than where I lived in San Francisco. If I could get to the $40,000–$50,000 range, I might be able to interest her in trading with me.

When I got the trailer, I texted her once again to let her know what I was working on. It was a trailer valued at $40,000 and it was in Canada. I had a good feeling.

## TRADE 28: OFF-THE-GRID TRAILER FOR A ...

Having the house offer in my back pocket gave me some extra security as I progressed through the trades. At the same time, it wasn't a sure thing. I didn't have paperwork signed or a written guarantee that Ciera would follow through. However, knowing that someone would even entertain the idea of trading me a house gave me a huge boost of confidence.

The trailer wasn't the first item I'd offered her. She had turned down a few trades, and there were a few I knew better than to offer her.

"God knows I don't want that Chipotle card," she'd told me.

Noted.

Maintaining contact with people who are interested in trading but not interested in the item you have at the time is important. There have been plenty of people who have rejected my current trade only to trade me for something in the future. Either I leapfrog to get them something they want or we reconnect several trades later when it's a better fit.

### Use Previous Connections

In sending thousands of messages during the course of the Trade Me Project, there are always people who "got away." By this, I mean the people who were very close to making a trade but decided it was not for them. In most of these cases, the person was probably open to making a trade (at least the idea of making a trade), but the item itself just wasn't the right fit. I like to take note and come back to these people in the future. Typically because of the nature of what I'm doing (trading up), I'll actually have something *more valuable* to offer them the second (or third) time I come back around.

When I got the off-the-grid trailer, I had a hunch Ciera would be interested.

"Yes!" she said. "This is great! I love this."

Knowing the off-the-grid trailer was going to net me a house is what kept me fighting so hard through the months—like six months—of trying to figure out how to import and move the trailer.

The trailer had briefly been parked in Seattle before the next mover could come get it for the final leg of the journey. On the day the trailer was supposed to be picked up from Seattle, I received a text from the driver that he could no longer come get it because he had totaled his car. It felt like we were *inching* toward the finish line. If I could just leap through all the red tape, bureaucratic hoops, and logistical nightmares, I'd get a house.

At least I hoped I'd get a house. I didn't have time to fly to Tennessee before moving the trailer. I shipped it directly to Ciera, trusting she'd follow through on the deal. The trailer left Seattle the last week of October and arrived in Tennessee on October 31, 2021.

Ciera and I went back and forth for several weeks while she decided which house she wanted to trade me. My only ask was that it was a house, not an apartment or a mobile home. (I'd spent so much time on these trades, I wanted to be sure I was truly going from a bobby pin to a HOUSE.) I was willing to put some work into the house, but I wanted

LET'S GIVE THIS HOUSE AWAY!

something solid, so a good inspection was also required before the trade handoff.

By mid-November, we'd finalized which house it would be. Ciera needed a few weeks to prepare the paperwork, and I made plans to fly to Tennessee shortly after the holidays.

Because I didn't have any signed paperwork or original content, I didn't want to announce anything on TikTok. What if I told everyone I had a house and then … I didn't have a house? The fallout would be worse than my Chipotle Celebrity Card experience, and I wasn't eager to relive that. But this was also a huge moment—the hugest moment! I wanted to make sure I had press there to cover the trade in the event it went through (which it had better!).

I started reaching out to all kinds of networks and outlets. I emailed hundreds of people saying, "Don't tell anyone, but I got the house." Before I announced the trade, 50 people knew it was happening.

Bobby and I flew to Tennessee on November 26, 2021. The morning we flew out of San Francisco, I couldn't believe it. We had to get up super early to fly to Nashville and then pick up our rental car to drive 40 minutes to Clarksville. The drive was lovely. It was the end of November, so the weather was chilly and clear, but all the trees were bare. A classic winter day in the South.

Our first stop was to meet up with Ciera and her husband, Bill, to hand over the keys. We were warmly welcomed into their home and spent time getting to know each other. It turns out they're passionate about philanthropy and believe in contributing to their community (especially to military families). Giving stuff away, even big stuff, wasn't at all out of character for them. It became so much more apparent to me why they were making this trade. They were just genuinely good people.

I asked if it was okay if we got the keys from them and saw the house on our own. I wanted to be able to have it just be me and Bobby (and Earl) the first time we saw it so my reaction could be as genuine and unguarded as possible. It felt like a rare private moment in what had been a very public experience. They fully understood and handed over the keys to us without further questions. I was so grateful.

Then we drove another 20 minutes to go see our new house.

OUR NEW HOUSE.

Bobby put the address into Google Maps and had me close my eyes while he drove up to the house. When the car stopped, he told me to open my eyes—and in that moment, I absolutely lost it. I went running to the front door and just *looked* at it.

"I can't believe this," I said, legitimately in shock. "A year and a half of trading a single bobby pin until I get a house"— the moment made me emotional—"and I've done it."

Bobby panned the camera over to the house. It was adorable. Small, compact, cute, and painted a bright sky blue.

"This just shows you—it's possible."

## Reflections on the Project

I didn't have much time before we leapt right into fixing the house up, but the enormity of what I'd done was starting to settle in. When I think about how I did this Project, the word that always comes up is *determination*. If you look it up, the definition is "firmness of purpose." That feels right. For me, this rock-solid sense of determination was ever present during the many months I worked on the Project.

This feeling of purpose was sometimes the only feeling I could feel. What do I mean by that? I've noticed that when people think about being "determined," they're sometimes referring to an activity, task, or purpose that takes an hour or a few days. For example, they were determined to clean out their garage or learn to play piano. It doesn't take over their life. But my determination felt all-consuming. Bobby actually calls this the "Demi Zone." I get this look in my eyes where I go into my own zone for days at a time, completely fixated on whatever it is I'm trying to do.

Even though my involvement with the Project was all-consuming, I also (and still do) work a full-time job in tech. I had (and still have) an agreement with any company I work for that I'm still able to work on side projects as long as I don't use company hardware, software, or time. The outcome of this is that any time that was previously free time was now Trade Me Project time.

This project took nearly every single free hour I had for a year and a half. There were periods of time where I wouldn't sleep well for a week because a specific trade (or lack thereof) would be playing and replaying in my head. Especially at night, I always felt like I was "just one message away" from finding a trade. If I just sent one more message or rethought my strategy one more time, I could maybe connect the dots before falling asleep. I'd lie in bed with the lights out (Bobby was always asleep) and turn my body strategically toward the wall with the phone at the lowest brightness so I could continue to work through trades until I eventually fell asleep.

Then, in the morning, I'd wake up to hundreds of people who'd replied "No" to my half-asleep trade offers. At night, I'd sometimes think of something great that would help me make the next trade. When that happened, most nights I wouldn't wake Bobby up to tell him. If the idea was amazing, though, there were other times I'd wake him up to let him know what I had come up with (I'm not sure he appreciated it, but he was always supportive of my 2 a.m. ideas—no matter how crazy). Most mornings, I'd wake up early and again lie in bed going through my phone until my first meeting for my "real job" began. It's fair to say I was obsessed.

I worked really hard to keep my work life and personal life separate. I think that's generally a good rule of thumb in life; especially once the Trade Me Project started, I wanted to make sure there was a clear division between the two. I'd done a pretty great job of keeping the Project under wraps until one day a coworker sent out a message to my entire team that he was cooking dinner and had TMZ on in the background. He recognized his "lovely product manager's voice" and ran over to the TV to learn all about my story. The cat was out of the bag.

I tried never to bring up the Trade Me Project at work. I wanted my "real work" to remain my "real work" and my "other work" to remain my "other work." Still, even with my effort, I'd always have a moment where people connected the dots, especially as the Project got more popular. I once had a candidate I was interviewing for my team who before I could even ask a question immediately had to mention they loved my content and they were so excited to be interviewed by me. It was so sweet and made me laugh.

For people who don't live and breathe San Francisco tech, my job as a product manager is to be the middle (wo)man between the engineers and designers. I'm the person who pitches ideas for new app features and then gets everyone on board to design and build it. To me, I'm good at my "real work" and my "other work" because both entail coming up with ideas that don't exist, pitching other people to believe in those ideas, negotiating when things don't go as planned, and then bringing the right people together to make those ideas a reality. There are apps and products you use every day that exist because of me—and to me, that's really cool. In this way, there's a real tie between the two spheres of my life.

One thing I found interesting during this journey was that the second people found out I was working my regular 9-to-5 and also doing my work on the Trade Me Project, their first question would be: So when are you quitting your real job? (This question was sometimes posed by fellow coworkers, which I always felt was pretty weird to ask.) My answer was always the same: There was never a single moment when I considered quitting either of my jobs. The feeling of the overwhelming challenge—the challenge of trading a bobby pin to a house or the challenge of somehow balancing a full-time job and also a social media empire—was half the fun.

I'm one of those people who thrives off busyness. The busier I am, the happier I am. In addition, the goal was to trade a bobby pin for a house, not generate a social media following. I never intended to become a social media influencer, especially one of those influencers who jet-sets full time, shares their life, and then opens free gifts from brands. I truly love and respect those people, but it's just not me. When I started the Trade Me Project, I always focused on the challenge of the project first; the sharing of it with people on social media came second.

I worked on the Trade Me Project by myself (with Bobby's help) even when I saw other influencers with much smaller followings hire an entire team to help them. I wanted to do it myself. By the time I hit 4 million followers, I finally hired an agent, but that relationship was never very successful. I realized with time that what I was doing on social media wasn't the "typical" influencer path. My management wanted me to talk about my daily routine, show my hair care products, or film what I eat for breakfast.

That didn't at all fit the mission I'd set out to accomplish. Again, for me it was the Trade Me Project first and social media second. I didn't want to show people my hair care routine (not that I even have a hair care routine) because that wasn't the purpose of the Project. While agents tried to push to show a more "well rounded" version of myself, what they didn't realize was that I really did consider *this* well rounded. Everything else in my life felt secondary to the progress of my journey.

I believe anyone can do what I did, but a crucial element is that overwhelming determination and focus. Anyone can dabble with trading (or even get really good at trying) without making it a fundamental part of their life. But trading a bobby pin for a house is a serious investment of energy, time, and life. As you can tell from this book, the Trade Me Project had some huge wins, but it also had some real dark times. Even during those dark times, when I was really down about finding a trade or getting to the end of the journey, my firmness of purpose was so overwhelming that there was no world where I'd allow myself to quit.

And no, the obsession didn't drop off after I had the deed for the house. I celebrated—but then I got back to work.

Just getting the house wasn't my final goal for the Project.

---

# CHAPTER 13

# THE TRADE ME PROJECT BECOMES A RENOVATION SHOW

We only had two days to spend in Tennessee before flying home. Those days were crazy. I shot a segment with *The Today Show* showing off the house and recounting the Trade Me Project journey. The segment was titled: WOMAN TRADES BOBBY PIN FOR HOUSE. Accurate but also hilarious.

Bobby and I also spent some time looking over the house to see what—if any—renovations it might need. When you walked in the front door of the house, you stepped right into the living room, which had nice hardwood floors. Off the living room was a kitchen with plenty of built-in cabinets and countertops. Then there was a hallway leading to two bedrooms, both with carpet and good-sized closets. The bathroom was definitely dated but still workable. The backyard was *huge*.

The paperwork was finalized on December 4, 2021. The house was officially mine.

Bobby and I had already decided that our next step was to move to Tennessee for the winter and oversee fixing up the house. It was in okay shape, but it definitely needed some love. We hoped most of our updates would be superficial. But we weren't renovating it for ourselves. We had decided we were going to fix it up … and give it away.

The idea of giving away the house had occurred to me pretty early in the Trade Me Project—maybe even back when I traded those first computers. I realized how much I had, that I was so privileged to work in tech, be economically stable, and not need to trade for a laptop in order to own one. Also, moving to Clarksville, Tennessee, didn't make sense. Bobby and I were happily settled in San Francisco. We had so much, and it only made sense to share.

We left San Francisco in early January with all our stuff— and Earl—in tow. The day after we arrived, I posted a video announcing I was going to trade the house. I wanted to change someone's life like the Trade Me Project has changed mine.

To give the house away, I asked people to share their stories—either on social media or with me personally via email. The stories I got were incredible. I got around 3,000 emails and videos, and they really ranged. The ones that stand out include a mom with kids who was sleeping in gas station bathrooms because the family was homeless or people living out of their car. Other people were undocumented and couldn't actually buy a house. I heard from so many teen and single moms who needed a safe place for their family.

I heard from the other half too. I got messages from investors who wanted a second property or people who wanted to Airbnb the house. These were financially savvy people who didn't necessarily need the house; they just wanted it. This stood in pretty stark contrast to the other messages I was receiving.

To process the applications, I read about 50 a night after work. I did this because not only was it time-consuming, but it was also emotionally draining to read all these tragic stories. I had folders on my computer desktop where I sorted the requests. The folders had labels like, "Maybe doesn't need house; will sell it" or "Absolutely not; financially stable" or "House isn't suitable" (this would happen when the family had six kids who couldn't fit in the house) or the person was homeless but not local and already connected to resources in their community.

I used the folders to try to sort through how I'd narrow down the scope. Finally, I had a cohort of people who seemed like a good fit for the house. I reached out to those people to get more clarity about their situation. If they'd just sent in a video, I asked them to write a letter (or vice versa) so I could compare everyone's situation on paper and on video. This was an amazing but huge responsibility I didn't take lightly.

Back in Tennessee, things were less glamorous. Between trading, renovating the house, choosing the recipient of the house, and working our two full-time jobs, Bobby and I realized we were strapped for time. We couldn't do this renovation on our own. We decided to hire a contractor, Shawn, who'd help us out. Shawn ended up donating not only a portion of his time but also funds to cover some of the projects in the house.

He also believed in the mission of the Trade Me Project and was a clutch addition to this final, critical step.

During the second week of renovating the house, we got a call from Shawn that he had bad news. While we thought we were just going to be painting and maybe replacing floors, the house's issues were way more serious. First, the framing that was keeping the house upright structurally had rotted where it met the foundation. Second, the floor was missing most of the joists that were supposed to support it. Third, the house flooded when it rained. We arrived to six inches of standing water. (Luckily, this ended up only being in the storage shed of the house, not the house itself.)

The contractor was going to have to jack up the entire house. This was way out of our budget. We told him to press pause. Was this the end? My intentions had been so good, but I couldn't have anticipated how much work my new house would require.

Then, 24 hours later, I got a call. Our contractor had called around and gotten people to donate some of their services to fix up the house.

I made sure to keep my followers updated at every step. Of course, when the extent of the house's issues became clear, the Internet was quick to point fingers. By this time, though, I was used to calling people out before they got too worked up. *No*, I explained, *this was no one's fault*. Ciera had never lived in the house, and the inspection had been clear. There wasn't anyone to blame.

While the renovations continued, I was still going through all the submissions I received for the house. While I was so grateful to everyone for sharing their story and I was close to choosing one out of the thousands I had gotten, I then received one email that stood out to me in particular.

Shay was a teenager living in Pennsylvania. She was 18 and living with a friend. When she was two years old, she had lost her mom in a car accident. Shay lived with her father until he passed away when she was 12. She then moved in with her grandparents, who relocated to a new spot.

Her grandfather passed away shortly after they moved, leaving her grandmother to take care of them. Her grandmother was physically disabled and was eventually moved to a rehabilitation center because of physical ailments. Shay continued to live in her grandmother's house with her uncle.

Shay stood out because the situation she was in wasn't about bad decisions she'd made but because of a situation she was placed in. It felt like, if anyone was going to use this house to change their life and get a fresh start, it would be Shay. She also didn't have kids or any existing ties that would make it hard to move. In addition, she'd told me she wasn't planning on selling the house; she wanted to live in it herself.

The entire time I was reading these submissions, my guiding principle had been: Will this house be the thing that changes someone's life? Of everyone I considered, I felt most strongly this would be true of Shay.

"One of the hardest things to do is ask for help," she said. She hadn't expected me to even respond.

On March 6, 2022, my mom and I flew to Pennsylvania to surprise her.

I'd told her she was in the Top 50 and asked for some of her personal information to "add to her file." Secretly, I was just using this to surprise her. I told her I wanted to set up a call with her as part of my process of going through the final 50. This way, I knew she'd be home.

First, I flew to DC, then my mom and I drove the four hours to Pennsylvania. I called, told her there was a package for her outside, and waited on her porch. She opened the door.

"We flew all the way here because I wanted to see you in person," I said, "and I'm here to tell you the house is yours."

"There's *no way!*" she said—and started crying.

I'd felt like I had to tell her in person. It was such a big thing and too personal to deliver the news over email or the phone. Plus, I just wanted to meet her. She'd impressed me so much with her tenacity and courage.

After we spent a little more time talking, we went and got pizza, hung out, and officially made our trade. I'd given the house away, but it would still be some time before the house was ready.

When I announced the winner of the house giveaway, people jumped in wanting to help. I set up a Cash App account for donations to Shay's college fund. People also asked if I could create an Amazon wishlist to help her furnish the house and send her off into her new life. Like I said, sometimes the Internet amplifies generosity in a pretty astounding way.

While press and conversation around the house giveaway picked up steam, the renovations at the house continued. In three months, we finished all the structural work and began on the fun stuff. We painted the house a lovely cappuccino color and put in brand new floors. We also totally redid the backyard. I can't tell you how much work this was.

By May, we'd finished almost everything in terms of renovations. The house had come with ancient wall heaters and no AC, so we installed a new heating and cooling unit. When the unit wouldn't fit through the attic, our amazing HVAC company, Mr. Cool, cut a hole in the side of the house and rented a rig to haul it up. We also fully redid the roof, installing new plywood decking and then laying down new shingles (thanks, Baker Roofing!). Our final project was redoing the siding, which was done by Helping His Hands, a volunteer group that rebuilds houses when people lose them. This house was going to be pristine.

One of the highlights was redoing the kitchen. It went from a full 70s-style kitchen with fake oak cabinets and dingy laminate floors to a bright, open floor plan kitchen with white subway tiles and gray marble counters. The bathroom was taken down to the studs, making it feel brand new. I also insisted on installing a stacked washer and dryer in the hall closet so the new owner could do their laundry at home instead of walking to the nearby laundromat.

The completion of the house was in large part because of our contractor, Shawn. He and his wife had a big role in making the house perfect. They were passionate about working on a house that was going to be given away. There were projects that just didn't make sense with our budget or that we didn't have much experience in managing, but Shawn went above and beyond to make it work.

The house looked amazing, but I didn't want to give Shay an empty house. That summer, I went to work on brand deals, getting Rugs.com to send rugs for all the rooms. Then I worked with ADT to install security in the house. Purple sent mattresses and bed frames for each of the bedrooms. Finally, using donations and the money I got from views, we also went to Target and bought every piece of furniture we thought she'd need.

In June, Shay graduated high school. Bobby and I drove up from Pennsylvania, where we were living at the time, to attend her graduation. Of everything I had accomplished with the Trade Me Project, the best part has been the connections I've formed with all kinds of people along the way.

In July 2022, Shay moved in to her new home—and the Trade Me Project was complete.

Oh, except there was one requirement for Shay getting the house: I was going to trade it to her for a bobby pin, which I'd take ... and start the entire Trade Me Project again.

# EPILOGUE

When I announced I was giving the house away only to restart the process, people thought I was crazy. I'd become the second person to start trading with a small, low-value item and end up with a house. But I wanted to be the first person to do it twice.

Fortunately, I was used to people thinking I was crazy.

My life of side hustles had turned into a permanent side hustle. I love trading, and even with all the challenges and heartache, I don't understand why more people don't try it. If you have an extra Peloton around, I can 100% find someone who will take it for an item of your choice. Isn't that the coolest thing ever?

I was burned out from what I was now calling Season 1 of the Trade Me Project, but I had to do it again. When I went to surprise Shay and tell her she got the house, I also had her grab a bobby pin, and we officially did our trade.

Starting over again was daunting, but my next trade was insane. In early January, I went on *The Ellen DeGeneres Show*. It was wild to fly to Los Angeles, get my hair and makeup done, and then be interviewed on live TV by Ellen. Then as our interview was wrapping up, she offered me my first trade of Season 2. A bobby pin for a pair of VIP tickets to the farewell season of her show.

I couldn't believe it. Even crazier, I heard after I went back to my dressing room, people started trading with each other in the audience. The Trade Me Project was having an impact beyond what I ever could've dreamed.

My goal with this book has been to not only share my story, but like the people in the audience at *Ellen* that day, I hope the story of the Trade Me Project inspires you to get out there and start trading (or whatever crazy goal you set out to achieve!). Trading challenges you to use all kinds of critical skill sets—psychological analysis, negotiation, market research, logistics, social media, DIY, and so on. My trading skills have translated to so many other aspects of my life.

As of the time of writing, I'm well into Season 2 of the Trade Me Project. This season has already had totally unexpected twists and turns. While my trading abilities are miles more sophisticated than they were when I first started out, the fun

("fun") part about trading is you can never predict what'll happen. Will I become the first person to trade all the way up from a bobby pin to a house twice?

Stay tuned …

# Trade Me Project: Season 1 Trades

| TRADE 1 | TRADE 2 | TRADE 3 | TRADE 4 |
|---|---|---|---|
| bobby pin | earrings | margarita glasses | vacuum |

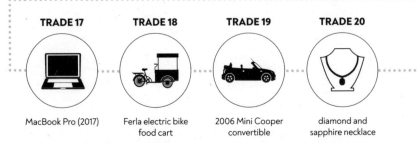

| TRADE 9 | TRADE 10 | TRADE 11 | TRADE 12 |
|---|---|---|---|
| MacBook Pro (2011) | Canon camera | Nike Blazers | Hyperdunks |

| TRADE 17 | TRADE 18 | TRADE 19 | TRADE 20 |
|---|---|---|---|
| MacBook Pro (2017) | Ferla electric bike food cart | 2006 Mini Cooper convertible | diamond and sapphire necklace |

| TRADE 25 | TRADE 26 | TRADE 27 | TRADE 28 |
|---|---|---|---|
| Honda CRV | tractors (x3) | Chipotle Celebrity Card | off-the-grid trailer |

### TRADE 5
snowboard

### TRADE 6
Apple TV 4K

### TRADE 7
Bose headphones

### TRADE 8
XBox One

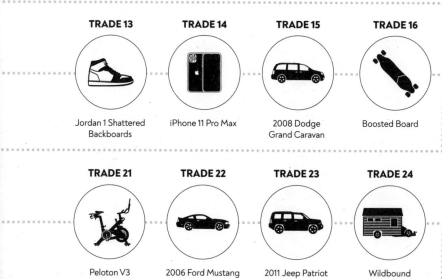

### TRADE 13
Jordan 1 Shattered
Backboards

### TRADE 14
iPhone 11 Pro Max

### TRADE 15
2008 Dodge
Grand Caravan

### TRADE 16
Boosted Board

### TRADE 21
Peloton V3

### TRADE 22
2006 Ford Mustang
GT Deluxe

### TRADE 23
2011 Jeep Patriot
Sport

### TRADE 24
Wildbound
Tiny Cabin

HOUSE!

# THE TRADE ME PROJECT'S

**Trading Handbook**

## A Guide to Getting Started

The Trade Me Project will always be one of my proudest accomplishments. In so many ways, it feels like something I was almost predestined to do—a project perfectly suited to all my strengths. To me, the Trade Me Project (and all its twists and turns) felt like second nature.

It wasn't until I began posting to TikTok that I realized what a mystery this type of project is for others. I've received hundreds of questions from followers asking about how I accomplished my goal and how they can start a trading project of their own.

*How can I start my own trading project?*

*Do I have to ask someone permission to begin?*

*What should I start with?*

*What tools and websites should I use?*

Questions like these are a big part of why this book (and particularly this handbook) came to exist. I held answers to all these questions, but I didn't have them written down and documented—but now I do.

If the story of the Trade Me Project has inspired you to start your own trading journey, this handbook contains all the tools and strategies you'll need—and it all starts with setting a goal.

## Define Your Goals

The first step in your trading journey should always be to set a goal. Having a goal at the outset will give you an anchor to keep going when trades are good and to continue pushing through when trades hit a roadblock.

Whether it's a small goal, like trading up to a PlayStation 5, or a large goal, like trading up to a house, the tips in this guide will help give you the step-by-step knowledge you need to successfully trade up to any goal!

## Choose Your Item

Now that you've decided on the goal you hope to achieve, its time to choose the item you want to start with. It might seem easier to start with a high-value item, but I urge you to start with something that has the value of a single penny.

Why? In starting with something that's valued at one penny, you'll not only learn a lot about what it takes to make a connection and complete a successful trade, but you'll also gain the positive momentum you'll need when your trading journey gets harder. While it might seem easier to start with a more valuable item, trying to trade something expensive will only paralyze you faster without allowing you to learn from the beginning.

Starting with something smaller also means you have less to lose.

If you start with a bobby pin, the worst thing that could happen is you lose your initial investment (the bobby pin). If you start with something larger, like an iPhone, the loss of your initial investment is much larger.

Trading takes some time to get used to, especially as you develop your own strategies and style. Start with low-stake items to give yourself lots of room to grow.

This first item could be anything you have in your own home, which also allows you to not spend a single cent from the get-go. Some useful examples could be:

- The trusty bobby pin (which I've tested myself, as you might have heard)

- The paper clip (tested successfully by Kyle MacDonald)

- Screws, nails, or household tools

- Pencils, pens, or things you buy in large quantities, which alone are valued at a single penny

## Choose a Platform

I have a lot of respect for people who traded in the pre-digital days. Whether it was going to a local barter market, listing your item in the newspaper, or calling people up via the yellow pages, it was certainly a mode of trading that required a lot of groundwork. The Internet has totally changed all that.

However, digitally enabled trading is kind of a double-edged sword. The ability to reach thousands of people and look through tens of thousands of items is a blessing and a curse. On one hand, list an item on one or several digital platforms and it will immediately be seen by an incredible number of people. On the other hand, you have to cut through all the noise. The same goes for finding an item you want, although we'll address that in depth later.

Every trade in the Trade Me Project started on the Internet, even if we later moved negotiations to the phone. Because of this, the most common question I'm asked about the Trade Me Project is what website I use to trade. Sadly, there isn't a dedicated "trading platform" with a large enough reach yet (although I've considered making one myself), but plenty of social media sites are great to leverage to make your trades:

- **Facebook Marketplace:** This platform for buying, selling, and trading is integrated into your Facebook account. While the platform has its own set of issues (e.g., it sets auto-replies for you that can kill trade momentum), the ability to search and filter across large geographic areas is beyond useful. For example, you can set a certain radius to trade within.

- **Facebook Groups:** This is another Facebook product I put to good use. When trying to "go deep," interest groups of any kind that have already formed can be extremely helpful. By using targeted interest groups, you can be sure the people you're reaching out to will absolutely be interested in the item you're offering. For example, when I had tractors to trade, I joined tractor appreciation groups. These communities have already self-organized—they're just waiting for you to find them.

- **Instagram:** Instagram is an unexpected dark horse in the digital trading platform contest. While this might sound a bit backward, many Instagram accounts exist purely to find users who are interested in buying the products they've posted photos of on their account. For example, sneakerheads often have Instagram accounts to buy and sell their shoes. Because of the nature of Instagram, many of the users following these accounts are also interested in shoes and can be contacted via their followers list.

For example, when I was trading sneakers, I not only reached out to the "business accounts" that were selling shoes but also to the thousands of people who were following those accounts. One helpful tip: Instagram sorts users' followers with the most recent followers at the top of the list, so you can be sure you're reaching out to the most active followers, who are more likely to want to trade for an item.

## Craft Your Listing

Creating an enticing listing for your item is one of the most important steps you'll take toward achieving your trading goals. Here are some tips to craft the best listing possible:

- **Take great pictures:** Well-lit photos that show all the important aspects of the item are a must. You don't need a fancy camera—your camera phone should work just fine. Make sure to capture your item from different angles and show any key pieces (e.g., cords or chargers) and the condition of the item .

- **Be thorough:** While you want to make sure your copy is readable and concise, you also want to make sure all the details are there. What does someone need to know about your item? Make? Model? Year? Condition? Think about how someone searching for this item would go about it. What key terms would they put in Google? Make sure those terms are in your listing—the subject and the description. Your item is great, but people have to be able to find it—and then know what they're looking at.

- **Sell—but don't lie:** From pictures to description, you want to show your item in the best possible light. However, you never want to misrepresent or lie. Your job is to help someone understand why they'd want exactly the item you have as it is, not overselling and overpromising. That doesn't mean you can't be persuasive. I always believed the people I was trading with were getting a great deal on an item they'd really want and use.

- **Price your item:** I know this sounds strange considering this is all about trading, but I'd occasionally list my item in a price range or with a price and then explain to anyone interested that I was interested in trading. You can state you want to trade outright or you can try this approach—just be ready to explain your thinking. Putting a value to your item will take some research, but it helps the other person have a frame of reference for value. Deciding on your price will be easy if there are many comparative items for sale. On the other hand, if you have the only item of this type on the market, then you get to set your price!

## Understand Your Item

Ninety percent of the time when I explain the Trade Me Project to someone, they immediately ask how I do it. While there are many strategies in finding and completing the perfect trade, one of the first rules is understanding what items you can trade.

Over time, I developed two main item categories that fundamentally dictated my approach each time. It was like a decision tree: If I had a Type A item, my tactics and strategy were totally different than if I had a Type B item. In addition, I learned that items from specific brands were much more tradable than unbranded items. Again, if your item falls into one of these categories, you're going to use a specific approach.

- **Type A vs. Type B Items:** While all items are "tradable" per se, there are items that are more tradable than others. So let's start with the basics. Items that have a large audience or those that can be used by everyone are more tradable. Really, there are two types of items: Those you can post anywhere online and know that many people would reach out to you with interest ("Type A" items) and items that if you posted anywhere online, no one would reach out with interest; instead, you'd have to go out and find that perfect person yourself ("Type B"). While Type B items are in fact tradable, they require a lot more work.

Let's look at a specific example: In one trade, I had a vacuum. This item was very clearly Type A—almost anyone could be interested in owning a vacuum. In another trade, I had an electric bike with a cart on the front. While this item was much, much more valuable than a vacuum, it was definitely a Type B. When I posted it to Facebook Marketplace, no one reached out. Instead, I had to go find the perfect person myself.

Knowing which type of item you have will dictate your trading strategy from the start. A Type A item requires a great, professional listing—and then you can hang back and wait for the interest to come to you. A Type B item might require a little more research to post, but then you'll need to do the work of finding your core demographic. Join Facebook Groups or search hashtags on Instagram. Your target market is out there, but you have to reach them. You'll also have to know how to talk about your item so people will be interested, which could require learning some terminology and lingo. (See my sneaker trades.)

- **Branded Items:** Another easy place to start is with brand-name items. Any item with a brand has already done half the work for you. By having a reputable brand associated with an item, the marketing is easy. When I say "brands," I'm sure you're immediately thinking about a Lamborghini, Tiffany's jewelry, or a Rolex—but the item doesn't have to be expensive or luxury for the brand to matter. Even a BIC pen—by the nature that it's a BIC—will be more tradable than just an average pen in your drawer. For example, I often trade Apple products because the branding around them is so strong. That brand awareness means people immediately know what I'm trading them. So the more important consideration becomes item condition and a great, detailed description.

## Creating Demand:
### FOCUS ON THE PERSON

While I've spoken about items you can't trade and items you can, the true strategy is finding the perfect *person* for the item you have. A fundamental aspect of my success with the Trade Me Project is I truly believe there's a person for every item in the world. I just need to find them.

THE TRADE ME PROJECT

The key with trading is not to become so obsessed with your item that you forget that someone else needs to love it too. There have been a few items I've traded for that I thought were *so cool*. I was personally obsessed—but that didn't mean anyone else was. The trades were a little more difficult because I had to find the few other people who'd also be obsessed.

I don't want to scare you away from trading niche items, but whenever you decide to trade an item, you must immediately think: Who would want this? And why?

- **Get in the other person's mindset:** I find many of my trades by first getting into the mind of a person who'd want the item. I try to figure out who they are and where they'd be so I can meet them where they are. Consider demographic factors, such as age, gender, location, income level, and more. I learned to get into the other person's mindset early on in the Trade Me Project.

  For example, in one of my trades, I had a pair of Nike Hyperdunks. I posted them on Facebook Marketplace and had no luck. Truly a Type B item. So I started to think about where the people who want these sneakers would be and joined hundreds of Facebook groups specifically for "sneakerheads." In these groups, I posted everything I knew about the shoes and started to even mimic the way people spoke about shoes in this group. I posted things like: "Size 9.5, Clean/OG All, H/O, Willing to trade."

  From there, I found people who seemed to be the best in the industry who'd be interested specifically in

Hyperdunks. I then went to their Instagram pages—not to message them but to message their followers, who might be interested in the shoes. In order to sell to sneakerheads, I had to be where the sneakerheads were and speak sneakerhead language. I had to learn what was important to them. Did they value condition? A certain color? Then I made sure my listing spoke to the essential qualities that would enable me to make the trade.

- **The perfect person exists—even for the most difficult item.** I've written a lot about how certain items attract a lot of broad attention, but the items that appeal to only a small group of people are worth trading too. These are some of my favorite trading scenarios; they just require a little extra legwork and patience.

One example where I found the perfect person was the trade I made for a minivan. Remember, I traded an iPhone 11 Pro Max (the newest at the time) for a minivan—but not just any minivan. The previous owner drove the minivan from Minnesota to San Francisco to make the trade. While the trade seemed perfect (maybe too good to be true), when I woke up the next morning and attempted to move the van, it was completely fried.

I knew most people wouldn't be interested in trading for a broken-down van—because tons of people came and looked at it and then left—but I ended up finding a priest who was looking for a van to drive to LA with his family. He also had a friend who was a mechanic. While he looked at the van, he FaceTimed his mechanic friend, who told him the fix was an easy one. He later traded me an electric skateboard (an amazing trade for him and a horrible one for me) and had the van up and running the same day.

He was the perfect person with the perfect set of circumstances for a van that had been a hard sell to anyone else. With difficult items, you can't get discouraged. Instead, get creative about why someone would want the item you have. Be extra proactive about reaching out and generating interest. Don't be shy! Remind yourself you have an amazing item—you're just trying to find it the perfect home.

## Making the Deal:
### QUALIFYING INTEREST
### AND NEGOTIATION STRATEGIES

I should preface my strategies with the fact that I've never gone to business school and have never worked in sales. I simply enjoy the challenge of a good negotiation and find that in fact, I'm really good at it. For example, as a 20-year-old, I negotiated a salary at Apple that was much more than twice my previous salary, convincing them they absolutely could not build their team without the skills I had at the price I wanted. It's just in my blood—and I go for it.

But you don't need to be born with a love of dealmaking to be great at trading. These are all learned strategies that just take practice and some grit. Here's what I've come up with after negotiating for years to make the best trades possible:

- **Be persistent:** By my count, I've sent around 300,000 messages to try to find the perfect trades. For every 100 messages I send, 99 of them are an absolute "No" and 1 might be a maybe. While this ratio might seem horrible for most, for me, even the "No"s are an invitation to negotiate. Just by answering my message, the other person gives me an opportunity to start a conversation and ask why they have their item, see if there are any other items they might be willing to trade for, and if there's any possible angle in which I could be the new owner of the item.

- **Figure out what the other party wants:** One strategy I use when negotiating (besides persistence) is understanding who the person I'm negotiating with is. I pride myself on having a really good sense of people, being able to understand how they feel with just a simple conversation.

  One example of this is when I traded a MacBook for an electric bike. I found the bike on Facebook Marketplace and messaged the owner, who immediately said he was not interested in trades and instead had to sell the bike. After some research, I came to find out that the owner of the bike wasn't actually the owner but rather an employee tasked with marketing the bikes by posting them all over Facebook Marketplace in different cities around the globe. (Don't ask me how I figured this out, but it involved LinkedIn, multi-city searches, and the white pages.) Once I knew this guy was actually an employee tasked with marketing, I got him on a phone call to explain that this trade would be much better than the sale of one bike. After probably five different calls with the employee as well as his CEO, I managed to convince them they needed a new laptop for an employee (it would not go to waste) and that by trading me, they'd be getting free marketing for their bikes on TikTok. Having figured out what was at the root of what they wanted, the trade was made.

- **Play leapfrog:** Another strategy I often use when negotiating is called the leapfrog. For example, if I reach out to someone who has a vacuum for sale for $15 and I ask to trade them a pair of earrings I currently have, they might immediately say "No." Instead of giving up, I ask them if there's an item they might be willing to trade for. In this case, they might say they weren't really considering a trade (they always say this), but now that they think about it, they need a set of drinking glasses. I then find a trade where I swap my earrings for drinking glasses and then trade the drinking glasses for the vacuum.

These are complicated trades to manage, but they're worth it. So many people are going to say "No" outright or never respond, so you have to take advantage when people are willing to have a conversation. That way, you can also narrow your search in terms of what you're looking for, giving you a clear path forward through at least your next two trades. Line up a future trade, then get the immediate trade done to get there.

- **Play to win—every time.** For me, every trade is an opportunity to negotiate—more specifically, an opportunity to win a negotiation. You can't be half-hearted or shy about trading. Sell hard and mean it every time. You're here to win!

## Closing the Deal

If you're stuck and you can't trade with anyone you know, spend money, or trade back, there are a few levers you can pull to still trade. Make the trade look more enticing by:

- **Finding ways to fix up the item yourself:** You can do this either by physically fixing the item yourself (i.e., removing the scuffs on an old vacuum) or making the item look better by taking better photos. People really underestimate the power of good photos! You can also learn more about the pros and cons of the item to describe it more accurately. Just because you posted the item with one listing doesn't mean you can't revise and improve it.

- **Managing the logistics:** One of the biggest levers you can pull is managing logistics that others might not want to deal with. For example, when trading someone a car for a boat, you can take care of all the logistical inconveniences it would take to have a boat sold, move the boat, negotiate a new car being bought, buying the car, managing the title, etc. By doing all the administrative and logistical work, you make it simple for them to say "Yes" to a trade. Their old boat is replaced by a (new to them) car, and they haven't had to lift a finger.

- **Managing the shipping:** Another headache of making trades, especially with larger items, is shipping an item or moving an item to another location. In offering to drive, ship, or move the item (as well as bringing the other end of the trade to them), you make it easier for them to say "Yes."

- **Marketing:** With the success of the Trade Me Project, I've been lucky enough to be able to pull this lever. For people with products or companies, the idea of being able to showcase the item, themselves, or their company within the Trade Me Project is often just enough to close the deal. Your platform might not be this big—or it might be much bigger—but think about ways you can leverage your influence and offer your own personal marketing as part of the deal. This can include reaching out to people in your network or cross-posting the item on multiple sites so it gets as many eyes on it as possible. The more awareness you have, the easier it is to close the deal.

## Beware of Scammers

I managed to make it through Season 1 of the Trade Me Project unscathed, but in Season 2, they finally got me. I made a trade for Apple AirPods Max and later discovered I had a really nice pair of fake headphones.

My best advice to avoid getting scammed is to do your research and trust your gut. Request serial numbers, call in expert opinions, get the item checked out, and research how items like the one you're trying to sell can be faked. Pay extra attention if you're dealing with an item category where fakes flood the market, like sneakers, handbags, or electronics.

The good news for item categories where fakes are popular is there are often verification services you can pay for that will analyze the item for you. I did this for the necklace I traded for (although that was a bad trade for a different reason) as well as some of the sneakers.

A different scenario is when the item isn't a fake—it's just in worse condition than you anticipated. I don't count this as being scammed. It's on you to request as much information about the characteristics and condition of the item before you make the trade.

Don't worry though—bad trades happen. Part of the fun of trading is figuring out how to get yourself out of the hole and back in action.

## Selecting the Perfect Next Item

When selecting the next item you'll be looking for to continue your trading journey, there are a few suggestions I can make:

- Always make sure you're looking at items that are at least 10% greater in value. As the value of your items go up, you can increase this percentage.

- Never select an item that's the "top of the market."

- Select Type A items if you can or items that are universally appealing rather than items that are unique, specific, collectible, etc., thereby limiting the target demographic.

- Don't select an item that's in the same category as the item you already have. For example, if you have a 2012 MacBook, no one's going to trade you a 2015 MacBook because it's too clear to the other person that they're going to be on the "losing end" of the deal. Look for something totally different.

These aren't hard and fast rules but are good tips to consider as you develop your own trading strategies and style.

## Refining Your Strategy

Once you've selected the item you'll be trading for, something you must understand throughout your trading journey is that your strategy will change—and if it doesn't, you won't be successful.

What do I mean by that?

At the beginning, your search can be "wide." When I say "wide," I mean wide in two areas:

- **Your item selection:** Because you have an item that's low in dollar value, the number of items that are greater than that value is manifold; therefore, you can choose nearly anything to trade for—and it will be a better trade. Think about a pencil. If you have a pencil, the number of items you'd be willing to accept that are "better" is vast. While strategy is still important, your risk of making a bad trade is much less.

- **Your trader pool:** Because you have an item that's low in dollar value, your trader pool is also large, meaning the number of people who'd be willing to give up an item is large. As the value of an item increases, there will be less people who'd be willing to make a trade. For lesser-value items, even if they make a "bad trade," what they'll lose is not that great in value. For example, if they trade a notebook for the pencil, the worst thing that will happen is they get a pencil and lose a notebook.

But as your journey in trading continues, you must change your strategy to increase your chances of making a successful trade. You can think about it like a fishing analogy. With lower-value items, you're fishing in a well-stocked pond.

With high-value items, you're fishing for very few fish in a giant ocean.

So how does your strategy have to change? As your pool gets smaller, it becomes more important to identify your "ideal" item or "ideal" category of items. If you continue to reach out to everyone about every item, you're going to burn yourself out. However, by identifying an ideal item, you can learn more about how you need to close the deal for that specific item.

If you're just trading one high-value item, then you'll need to be especially careful and selective about how you're approaching your trade. Make sure you do all your research— think hard about what items you'd be willing to accept in this one-off.

## Getting Unblocked

If you're on a trading journey, you'll inevitably make a "bad" trade or even one for an item that's hard to find someone for. All is not lost—there are things you can do to unblock yourself:

- **Change your "ideal item"**: You might have overvalued your item, meaning that when you reach out to 100 people, more than 80% immediately say "No." If you're getting immediate and overwhelming negative responses, the item you have isn't worth the amount you're looking to trade it for. You need to adjust your expectations and look for trades at a lower value.

- **Change your location:** The location in which you're searching for a trade sometimes doesn't value the type of item you have. For example, when I have a MacBook to trade, I often try to stay away from big cities where people will get laptops for free from their company. If people feel like they already have the opportunity to get an item for free or already have too many of an item, they won't see the value in giving something up to get another one. Also, because I have the freedom to travel or ship items, it's not the end of the world to move locations. In addition, geographies that have lots of one kind of item (i.e., ski gear in a mountain town or water recreation equipment in a beach town) can impact the desirability of your item.

- **Change platforms:** My platform of choice is usually Facebook Marketplace, mostly because of the sheer number of users and the ability to search, sort, and filter. I'll often try to go one level deeper to Facebook Groups, where users have self-congregated, such as John Deere tractor lovers. By seeking out where my target demographic is already gathering, I can be sure I'm reaching out to people who'll definitely be interested in the item I have.

However, patience is key. Difficult trades can take a long time to get done—months even. When it all comes together, though, there's no better feeling. Keep going!

## Enlisting Help

As we grow up, we're told not to trust strangers. You learn to look at someone who's not your immediate family or friend with uneasiness; trusting a stranger could result in horrible circumstances. One of my favorite lessons from the Trade Me Project is how wrong this advice is. As Mr. Rogers says, helpers are everywhere—you just have to find them.

Time and time again during the Project, I was lent a serious helping hand by someone I'd never met just out of the goodness of their heart. I never regretted leaning on strangers. People came through for the Project and me over and over. Obviously, I was smart about it. I looked people up and made sure to get them on the phone before just blindly trusting anyone. I can say, though, that I wouldn't have made it across the finish line without the generous support of others.

Help from strangers was critical in the high-value trades, but I used helpers in the lower-value trades too. You don't need to be trading cars to call in a friend or a friendly stranger:

- **Helpers provide logistical support:** One example of this kind of help was a trade I made from Virginia to North Carolina. The item I had was in Virginia and the item I was trading it for was in North Carolina. Because it was the height of the pandemic, I couldn't travel and instead posted all over the Internet asking if someone could help me drive a car from VA to NC (a total of five hours). What happened next was amazing. Within 48 hours, I was able to find three women who all volunteered to drive 90 minutes and then drop the car off with the next person, who'd meet them and then drive the next 90 minutes until the car arrived safely at its destination. The car was successfully delivered within five hours, and I was able to make my next trade.

- **Use your helpers' expertise and credibility.** During my first sneaker trades (there were three total), I traded with someone who seemed to know a lot about shoes. So after successfully making the trade, I told him about the journey and that if he was willing, I'd love to be able to ask him questions about the next few shoes I was going to trade. He agreed and later was able to help me navigate the world of shoe trades (which are typically surrounded by people trying to scam for fake shoes). He was able to confirm the legitimacy of all my shoes as well as the values so I could continue on with my trades.

- **Small tasks are great for helpers too.** Other times, people even volunteered to store trades in their garages, jump car batteries that died, etc. It's incredible what people are willing to do just out of kindness and interest.

- **Thanking helpers.** Show your gratitude! If someone lends you a hand, make sure you thank them. Heartfelt thanks is enough, but I sometimes took the extra step of sending cards, gifts, or social media shout-outs. All the Project's helpers deserved the credit for the amazing role they played in getting the trades done.

## Final Advice

- **This is hard:** If trading, especially trading with a big goal, was easy, everyone would be trading their bobby pins for a new house. Trading isn't for the faint of heart. When you get stuck (which you absolutely will), try to think about the problem in a different way to get unstuck.

- **People will doubt you:** This journey isn't a conventional one. When other people express doubt about whether the time and effort you're putting in is worth it, remember why you started the process in the first place and keep pushing.

- **You'll get 1000 "No"s:** The good news is, for every 1,000 "No"s, there's a single "Yes" out there waiting for you.

- **Be strategic:** Take every conversation you have slowly and methodically. With every interaction, even if it doesn't result in a trade, you'll learn something that will help you in your next conversation. (And trust me, you'll have thousands of them.)

- **People aren't lucky:** After two years of trading and continuously saying "I'm just lucky," I've finally realized that people make their own luck. Luck isn't something that just appears for certain people and not for others. While I do agree that some people are born into better situations than others, luck is built on the ability to be persistent enough to know when an opportunity presents itself.

# Acknowledgments

Both the Trade Me Project and this book would not have been possible without the support of many people who helped along the way.

To Abbie: Thank you for making that very first trade. Your belief in me and the journey allowed this project to be possible.

To the Trade Me Project family (of which there are now more than 5 million): Thank you for following me from the beginning and for your support through even the darkest of trades.

To Kelsey: Thank you for bringing this book to life, and for the many, many hours spent documenting every detail of the Trade Me Project journey.

To my family and friends: Thank you for always putting up with my wildest ideas and for always believing I can accomplish them.

# Index

# About the Author

Demi Skipper is a serial entrepreneur from San Francisco who truly believes any goal is achievable. By day, she is a product manager at a large tech company and by night, she runs the social media platform @TradeMeProject with more than 5 million followers. There is never a moment when Demi isn't working on "her next big project," so stay tuned.